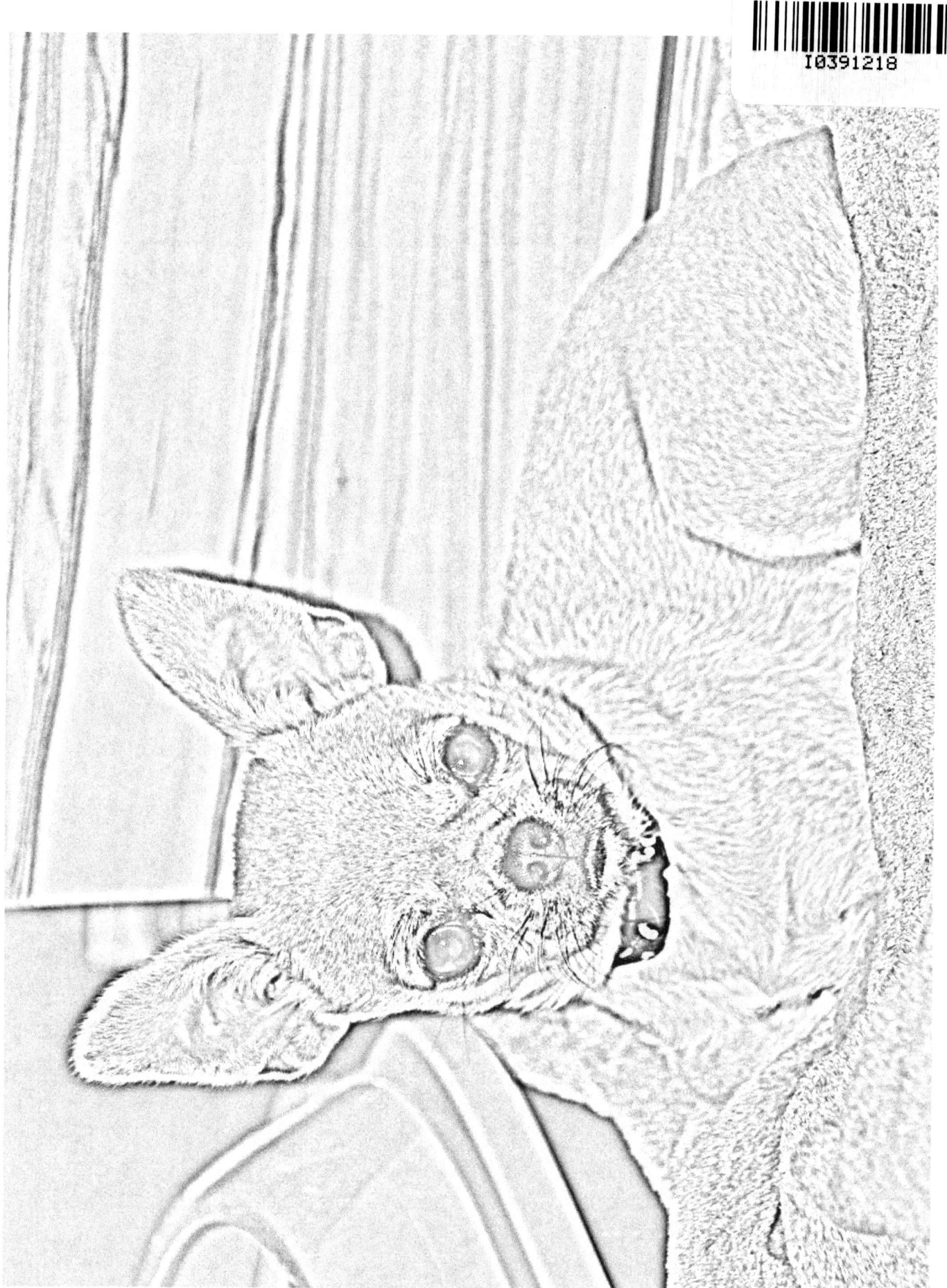

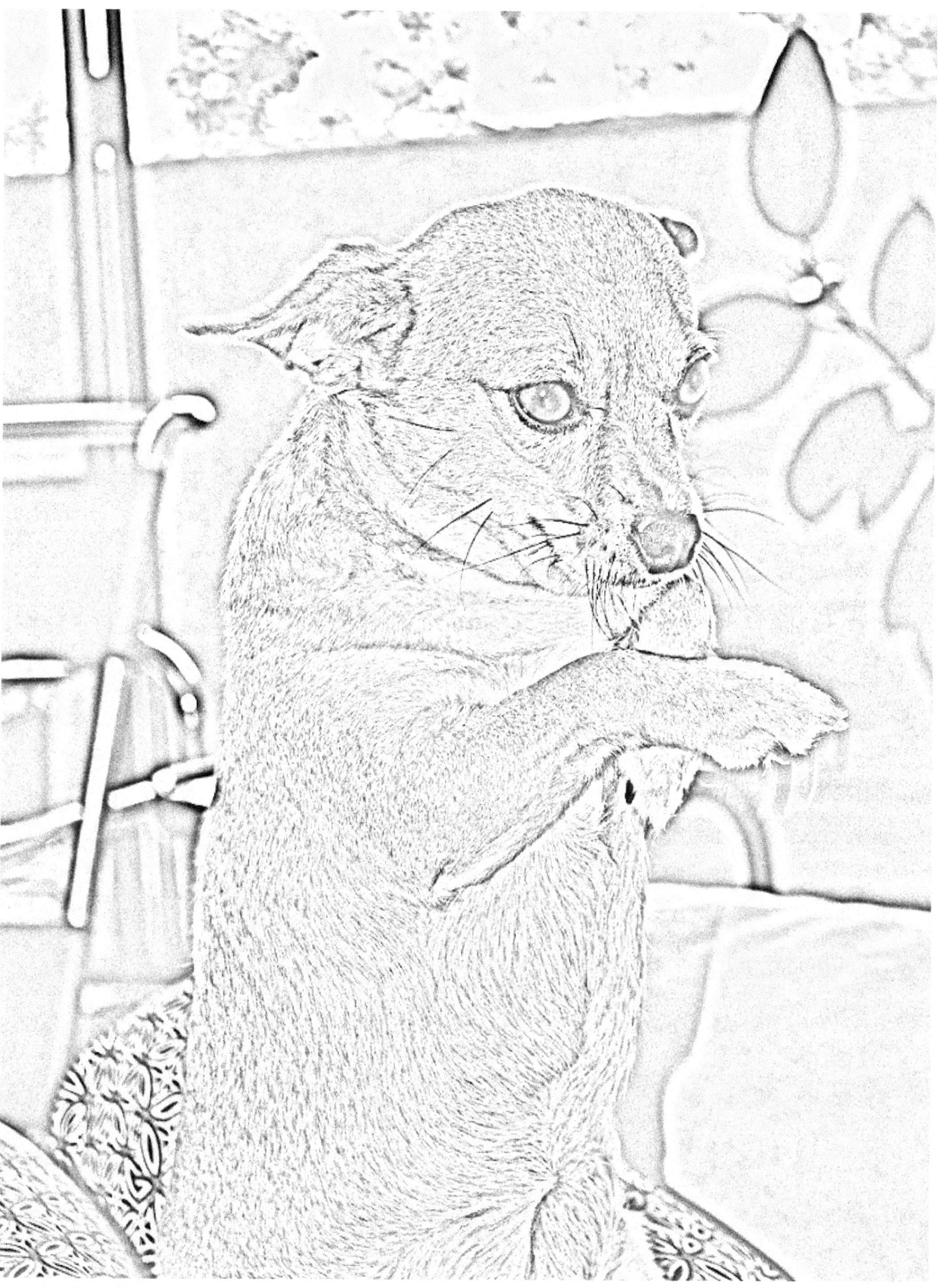

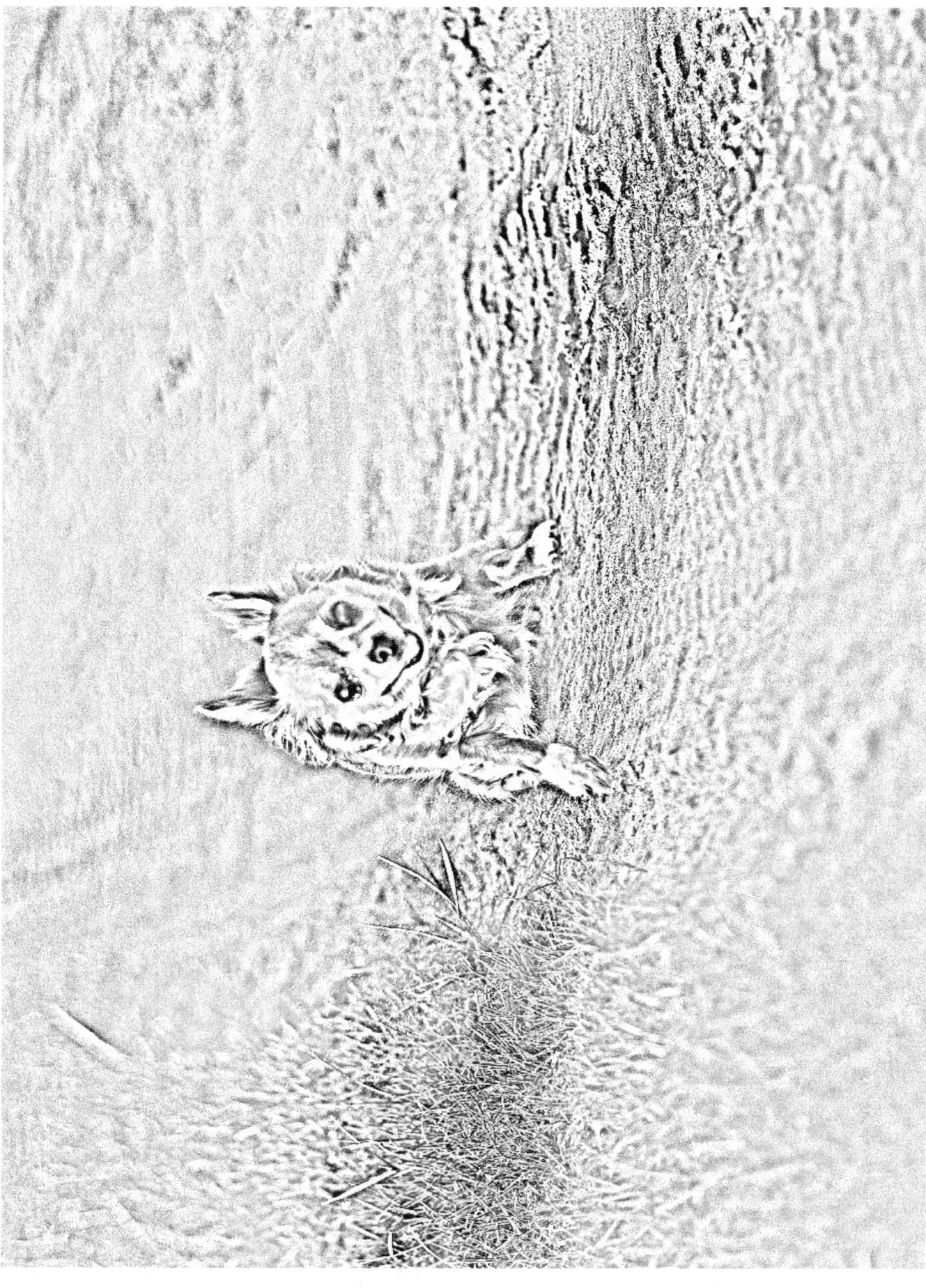

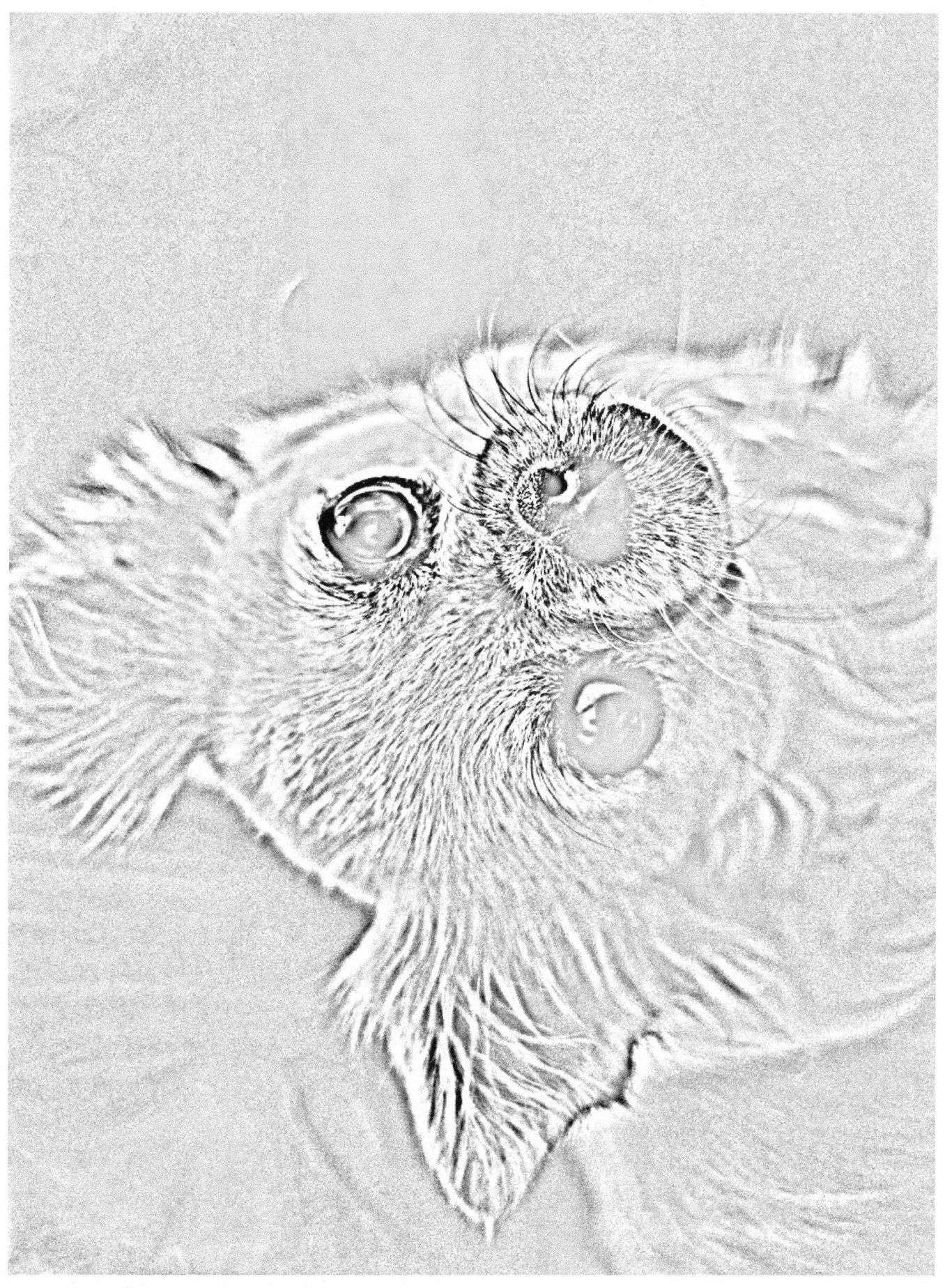

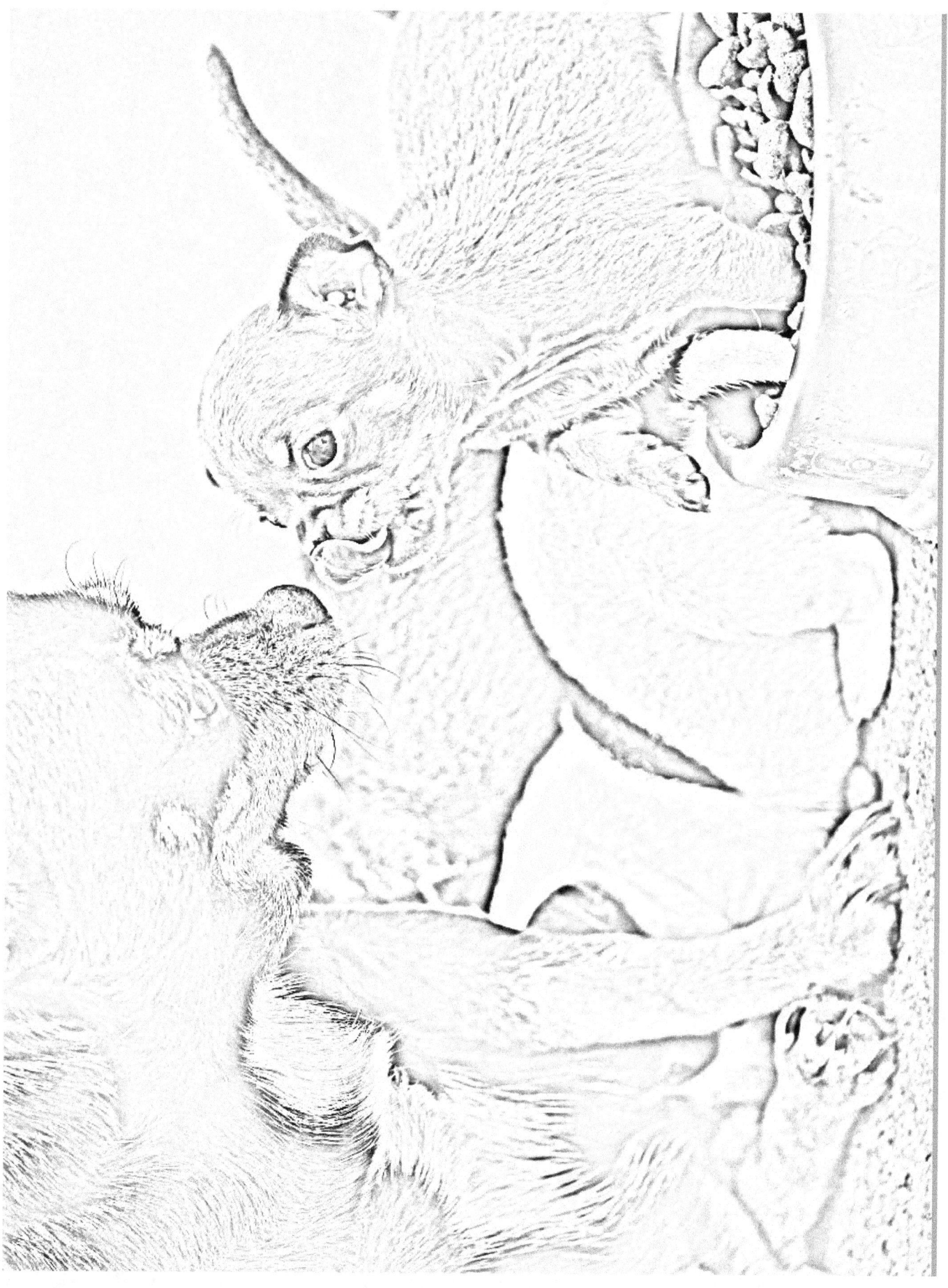

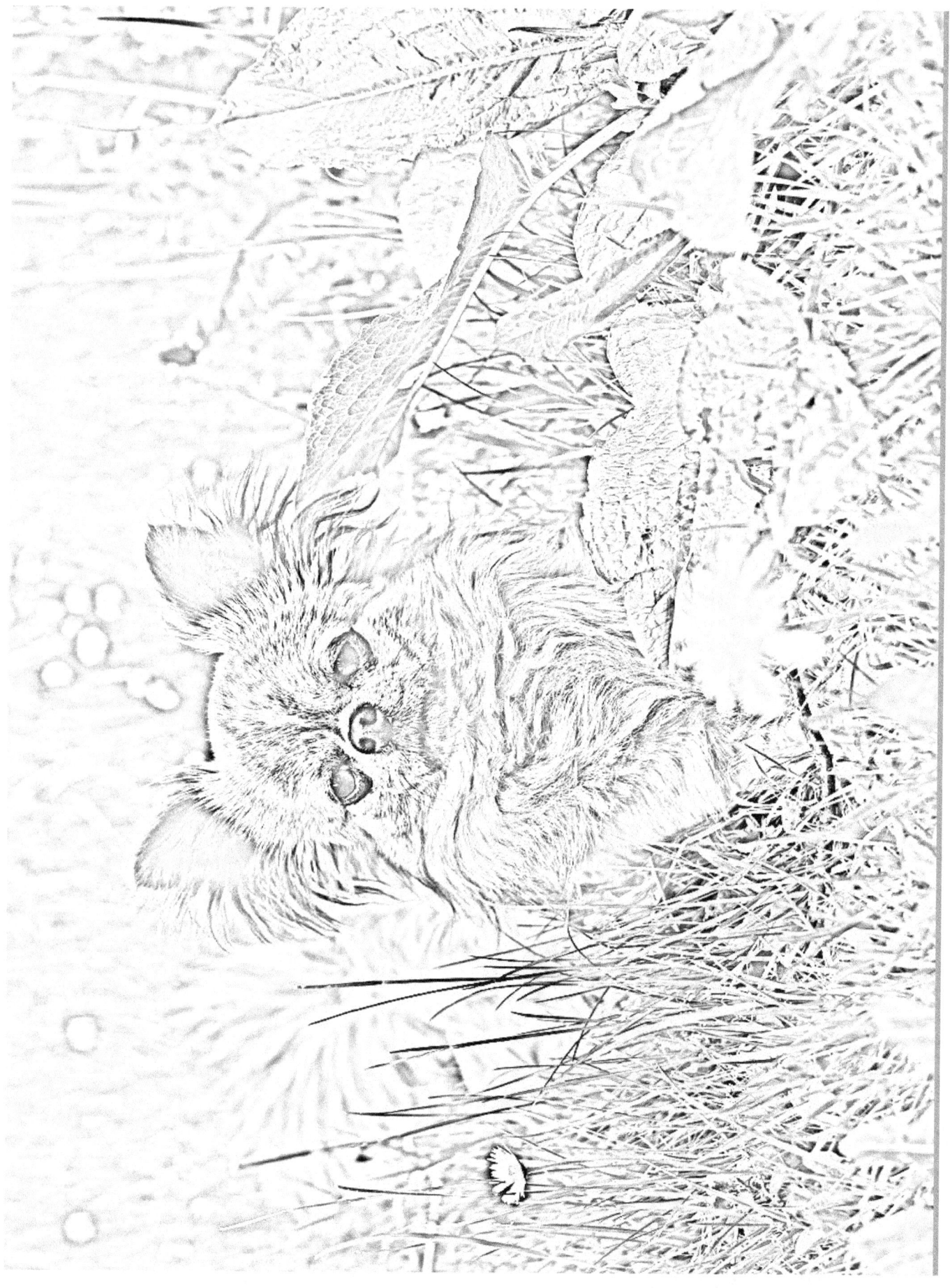

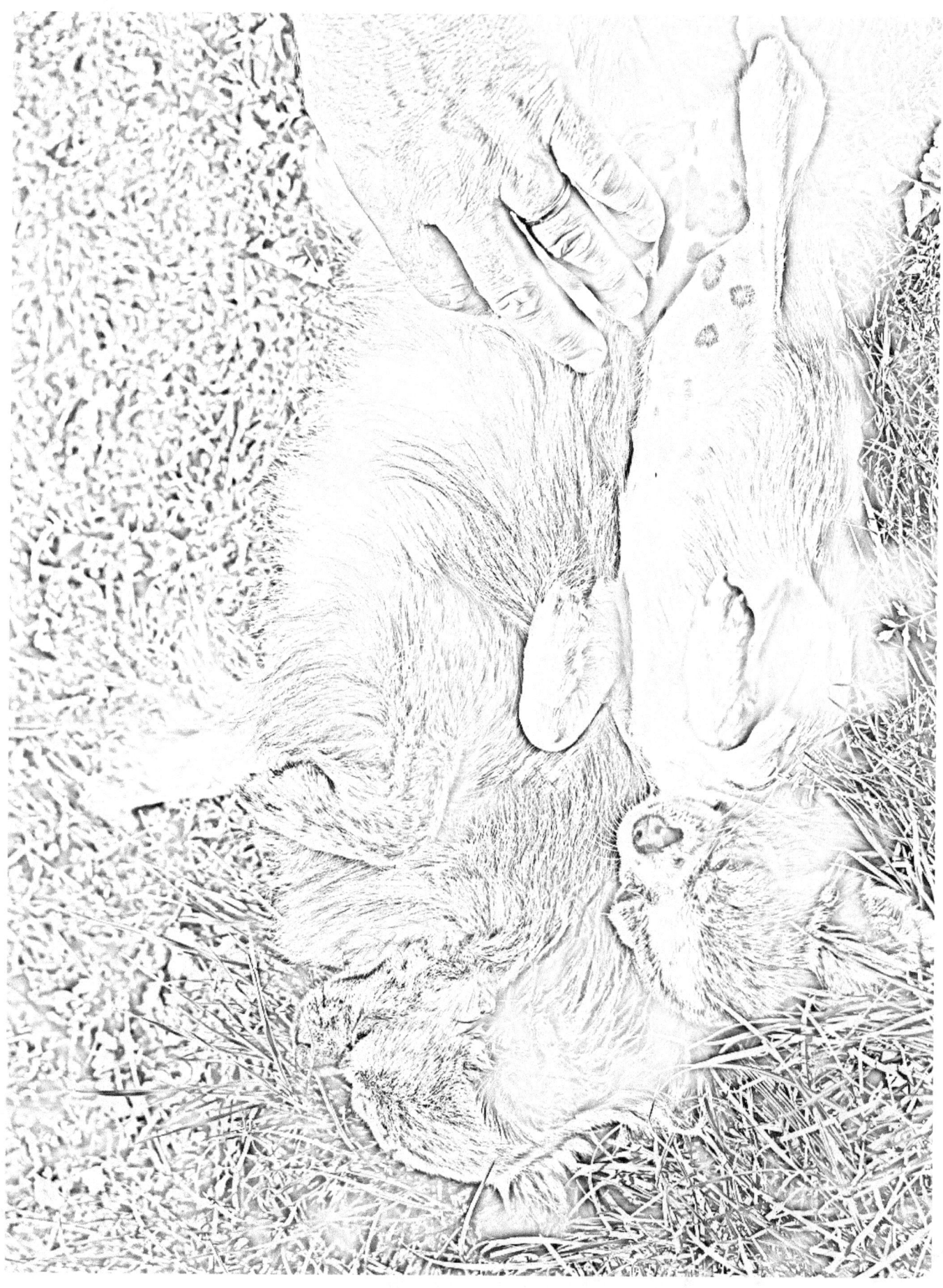

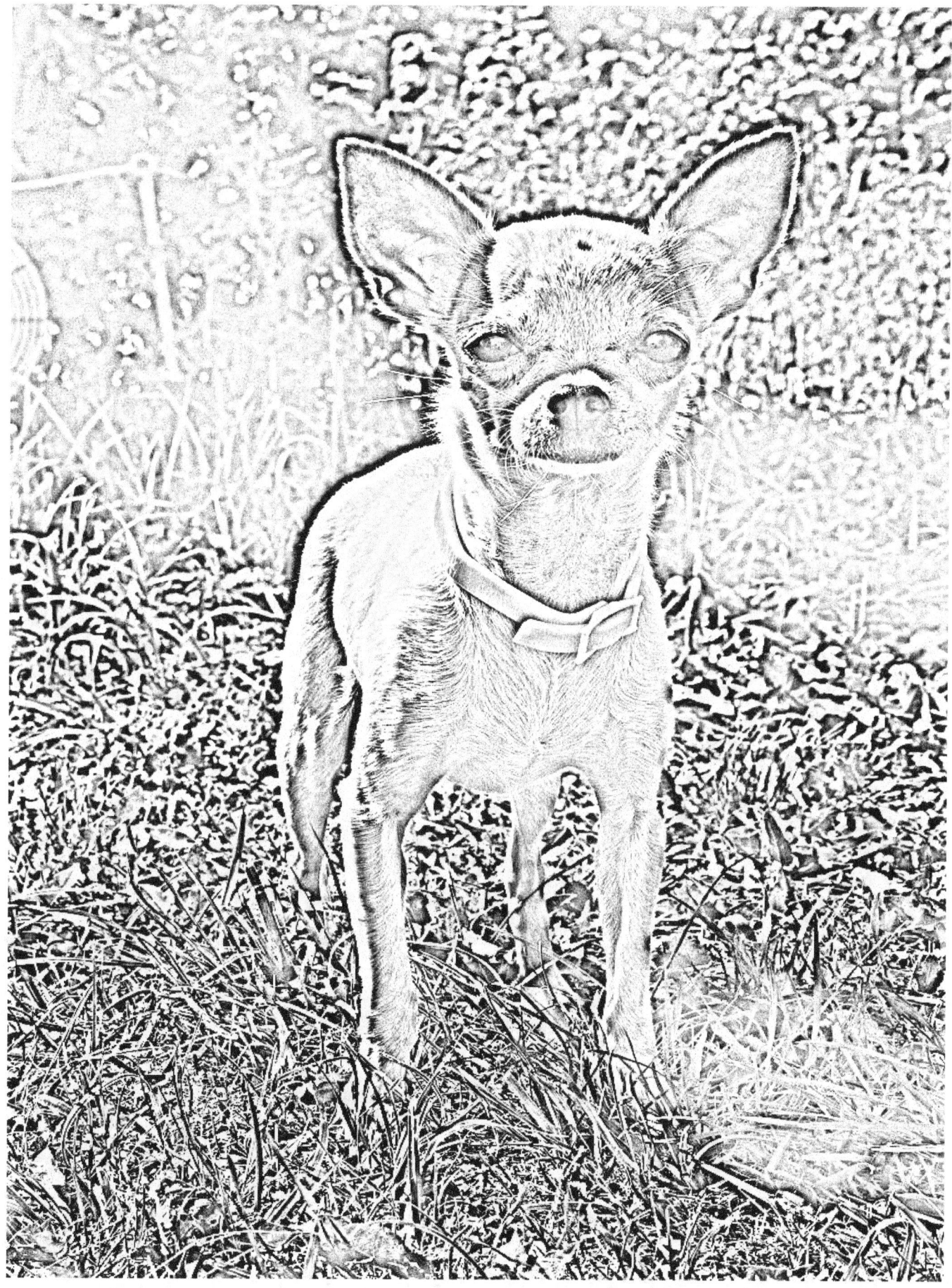

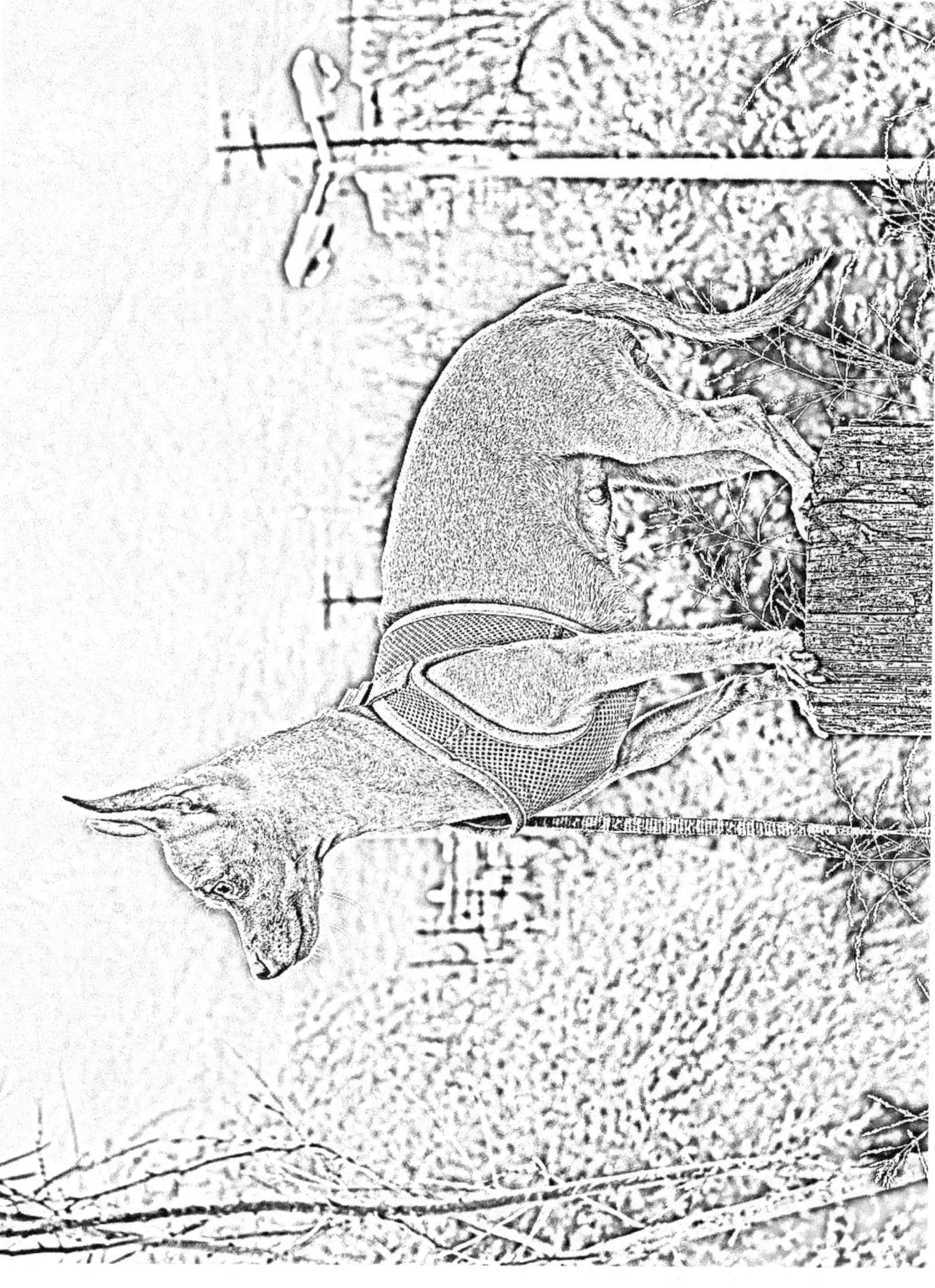

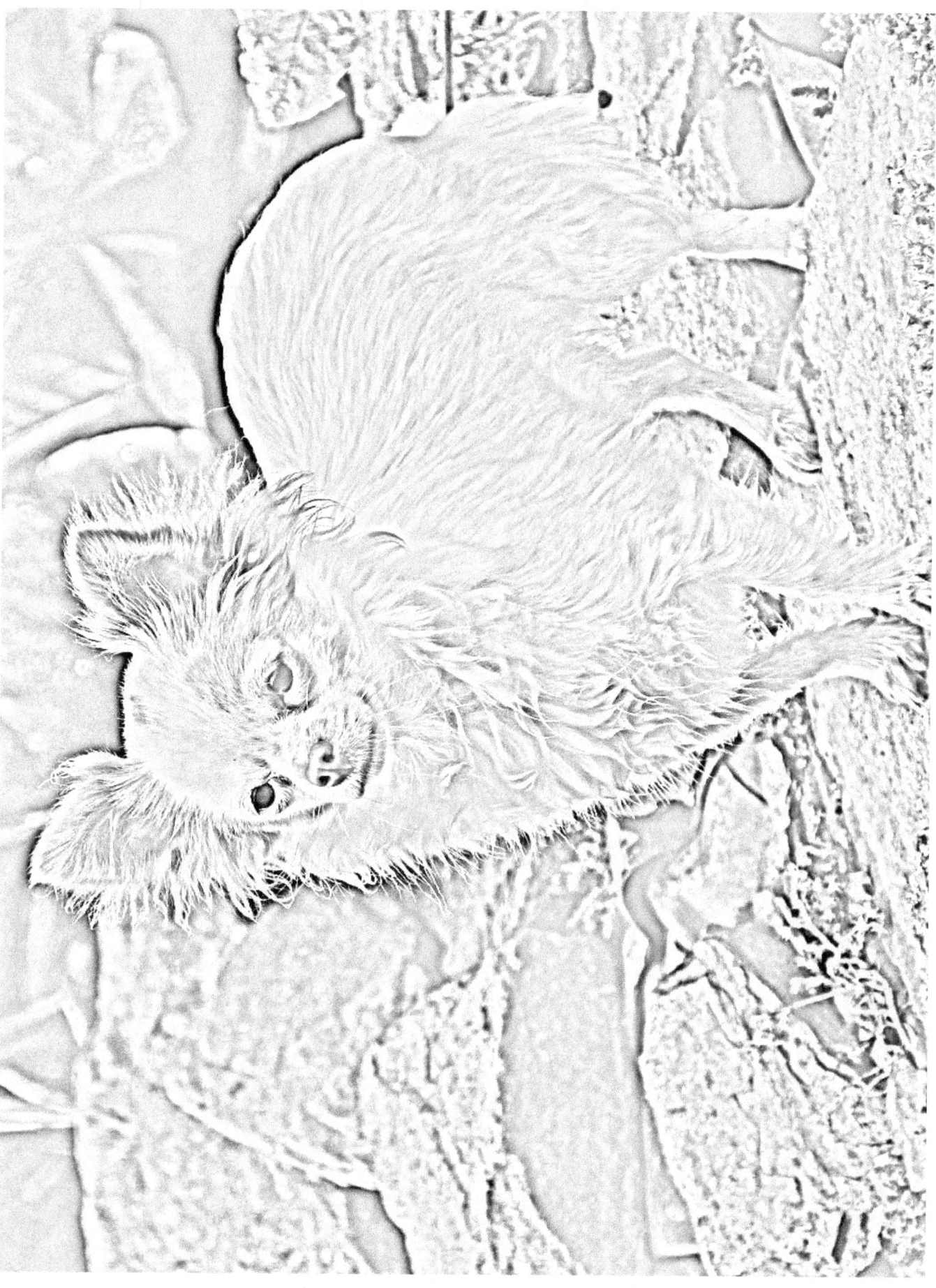

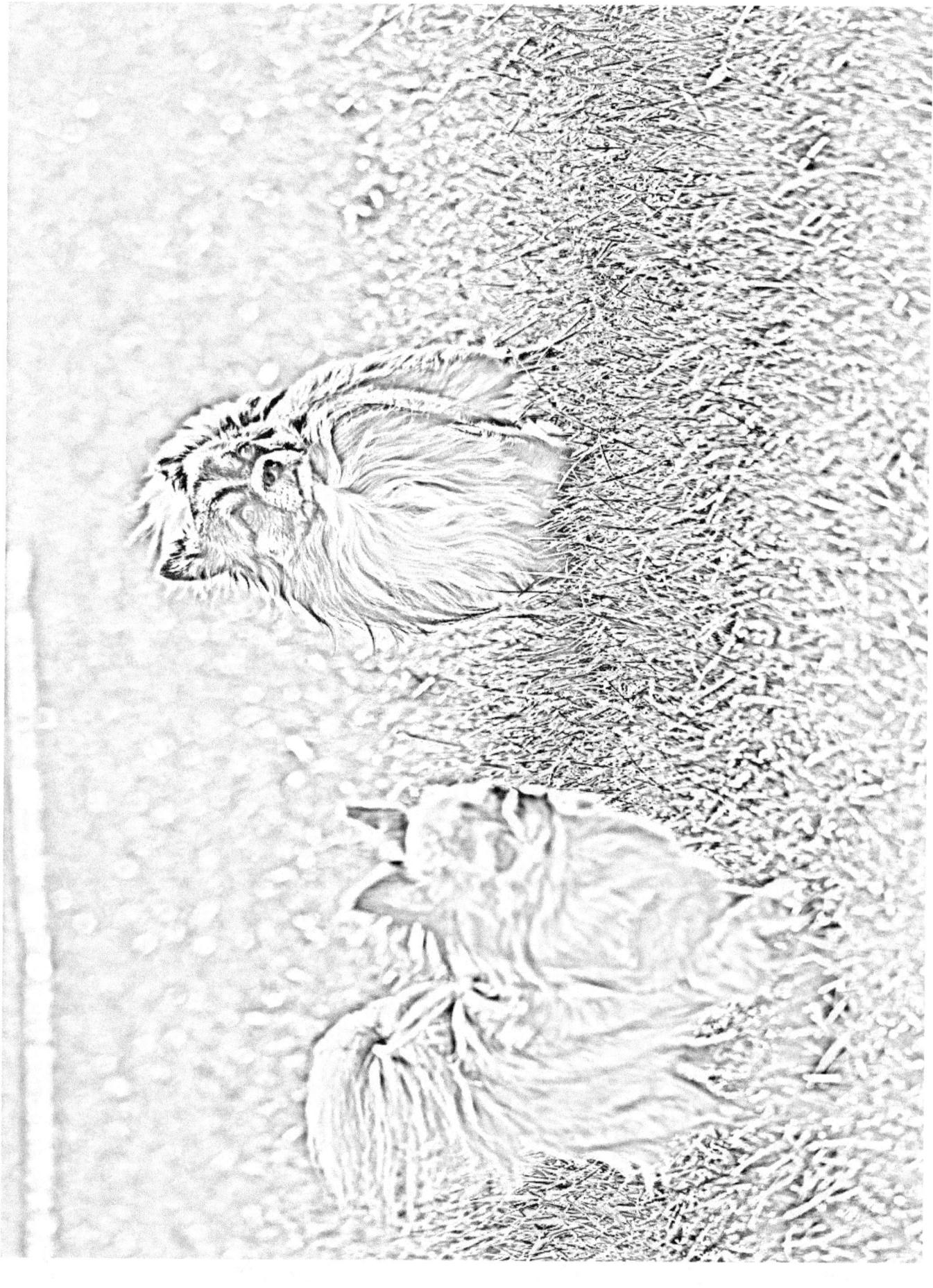

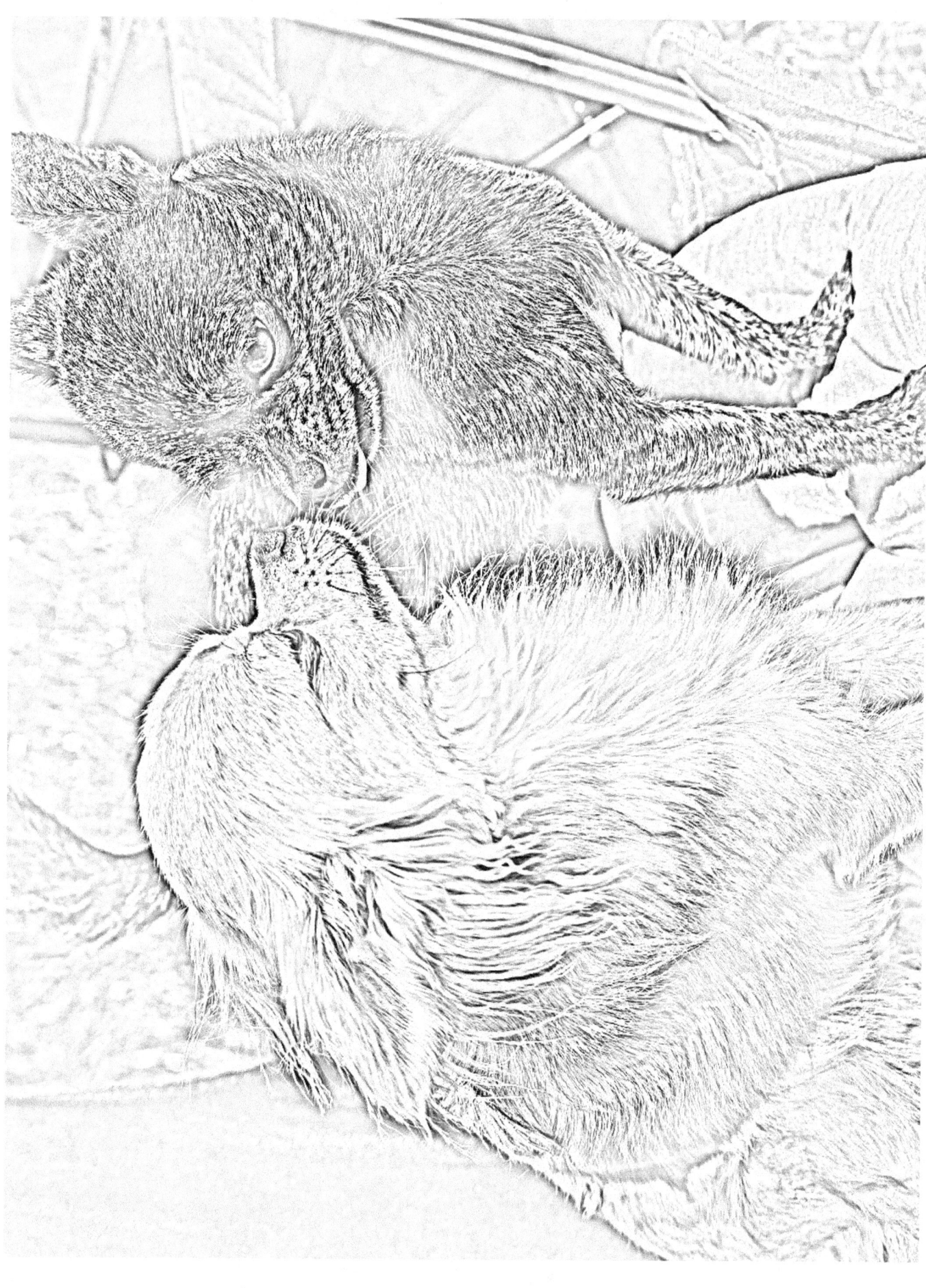

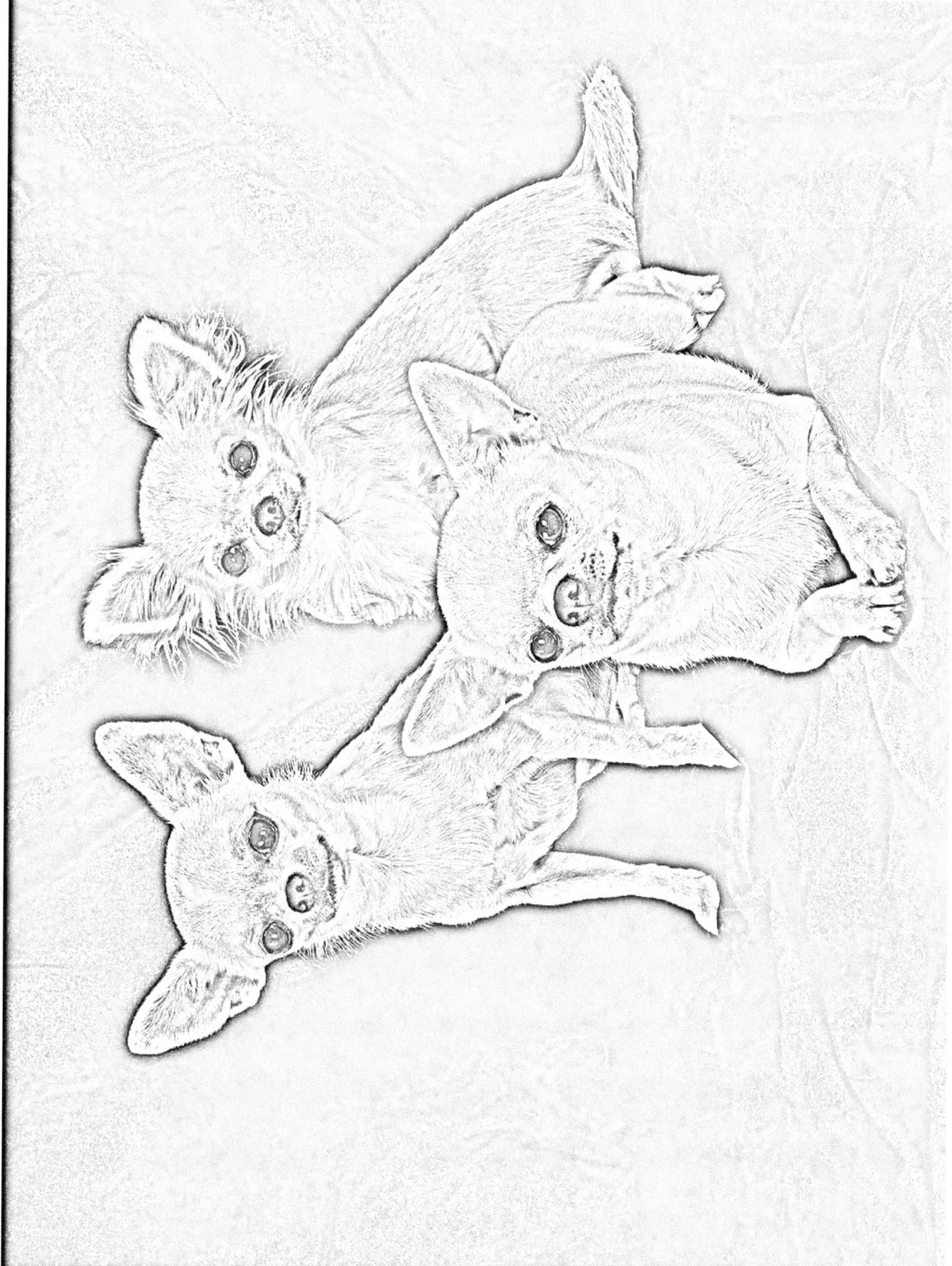

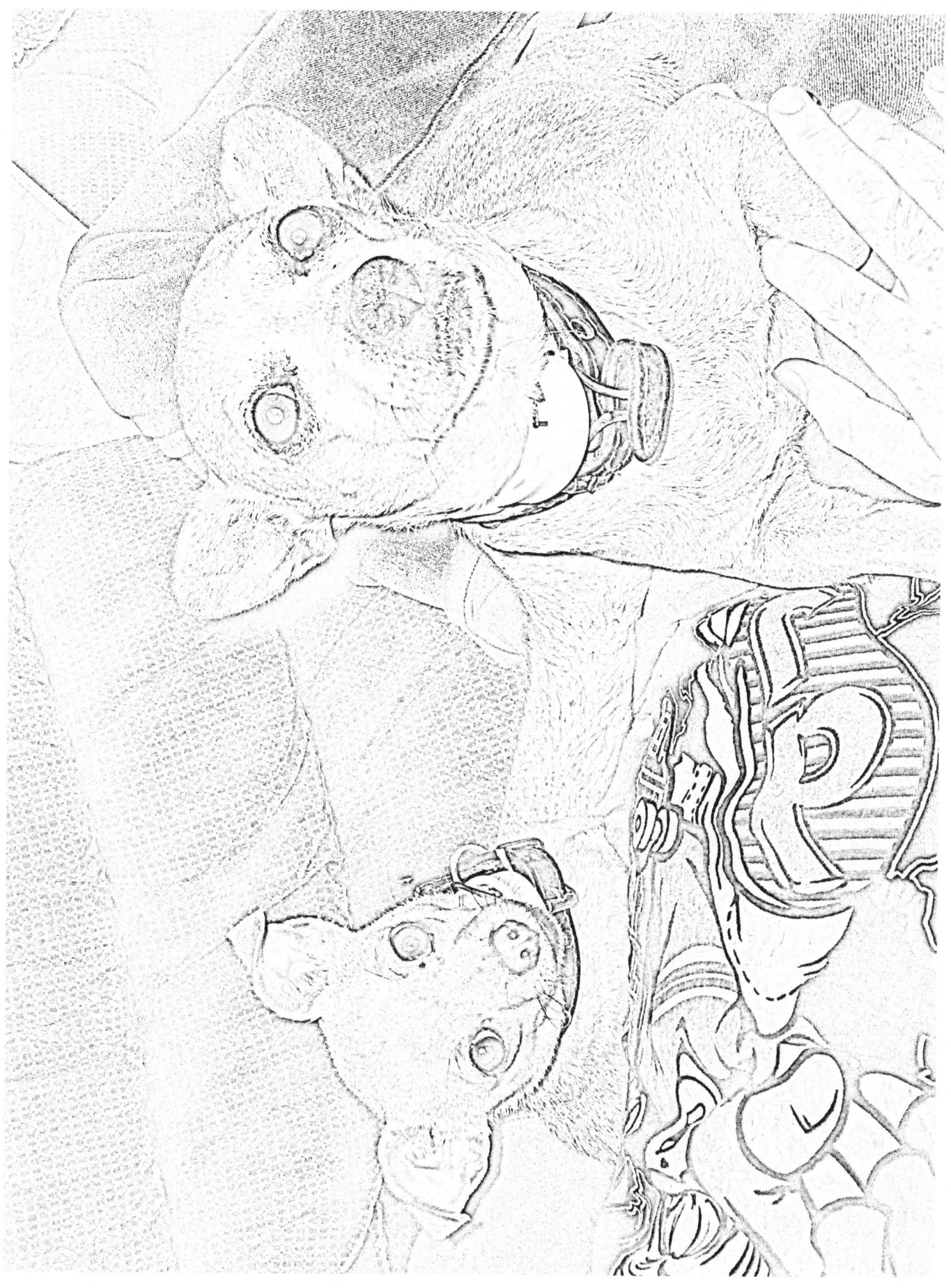

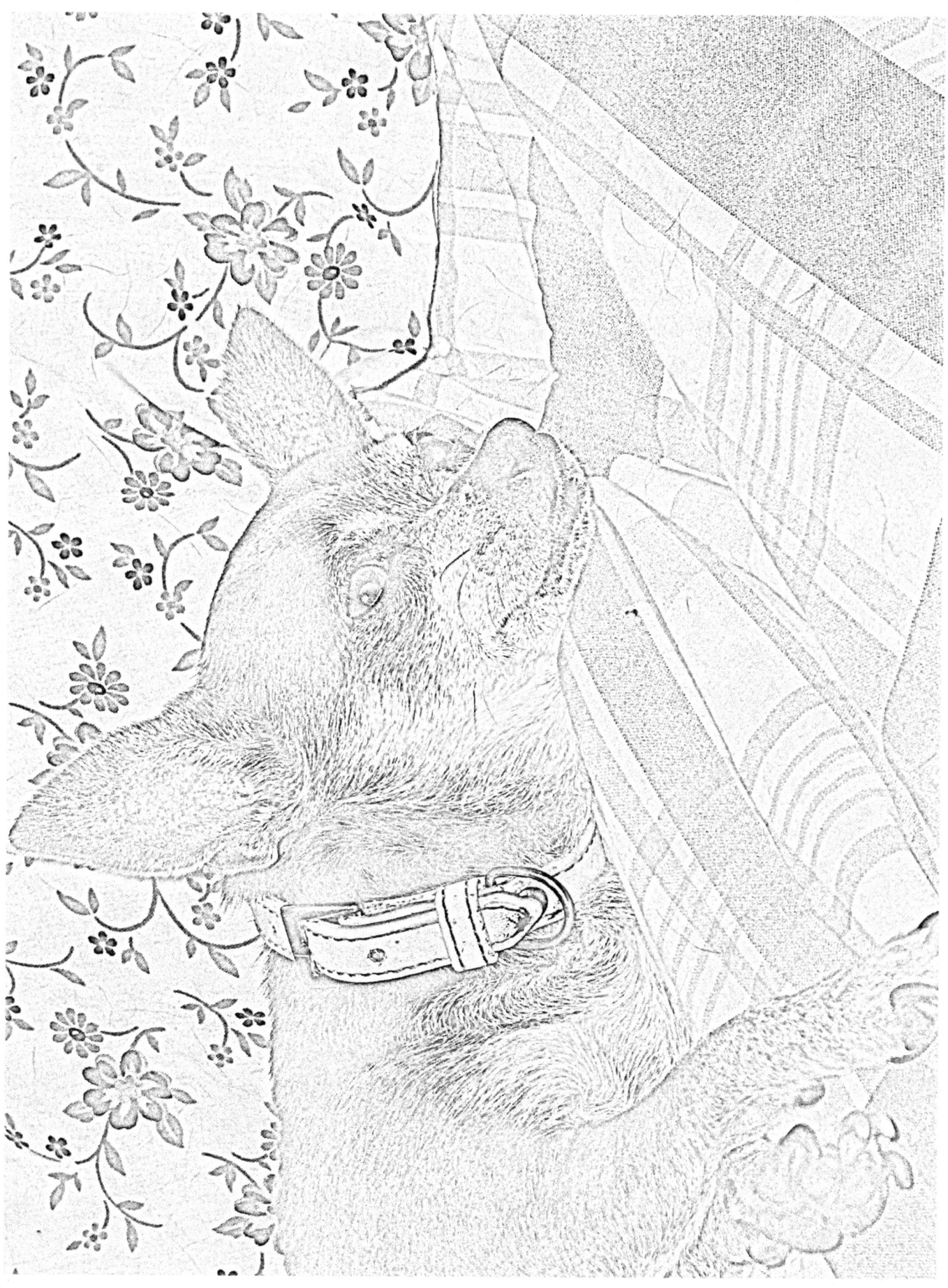

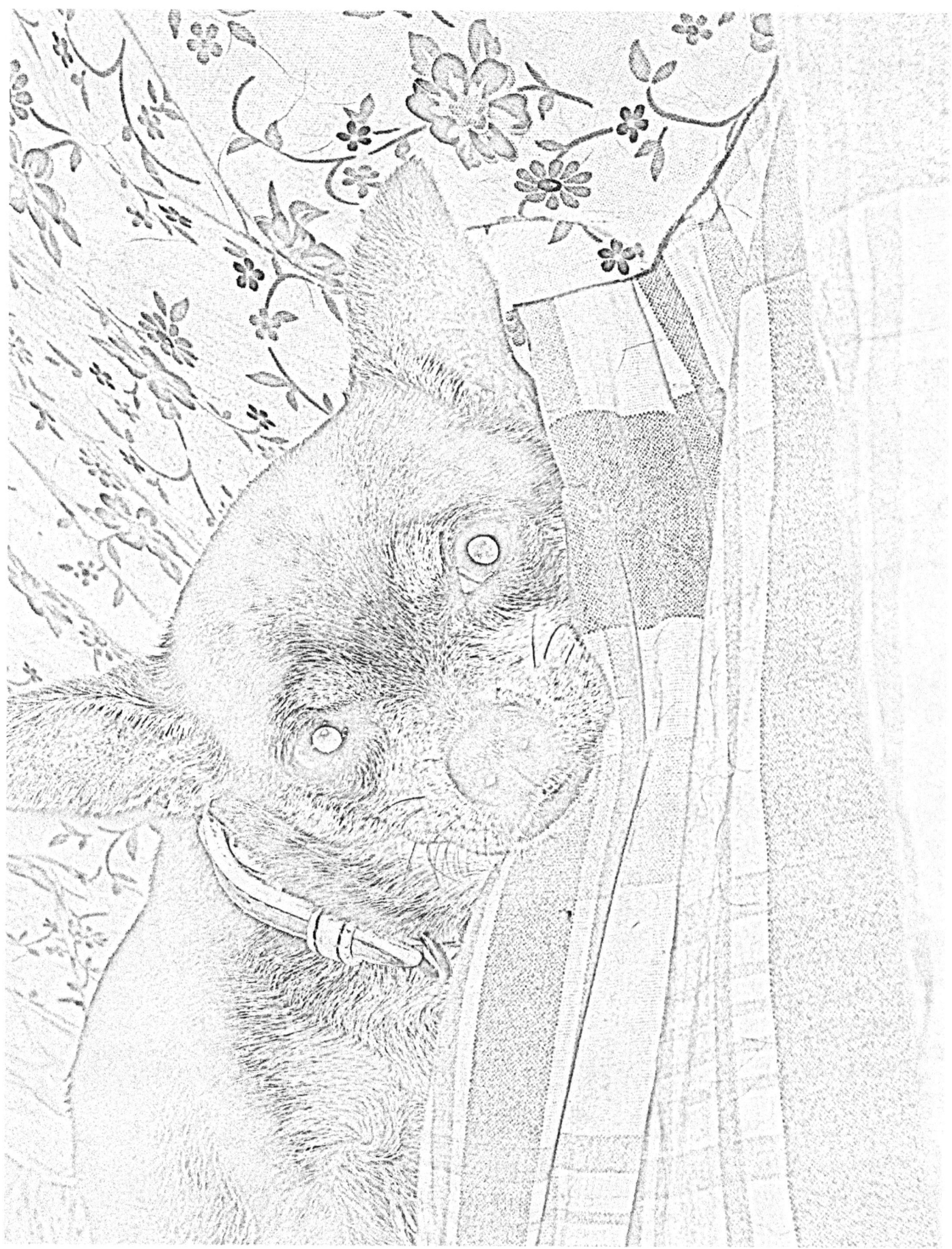

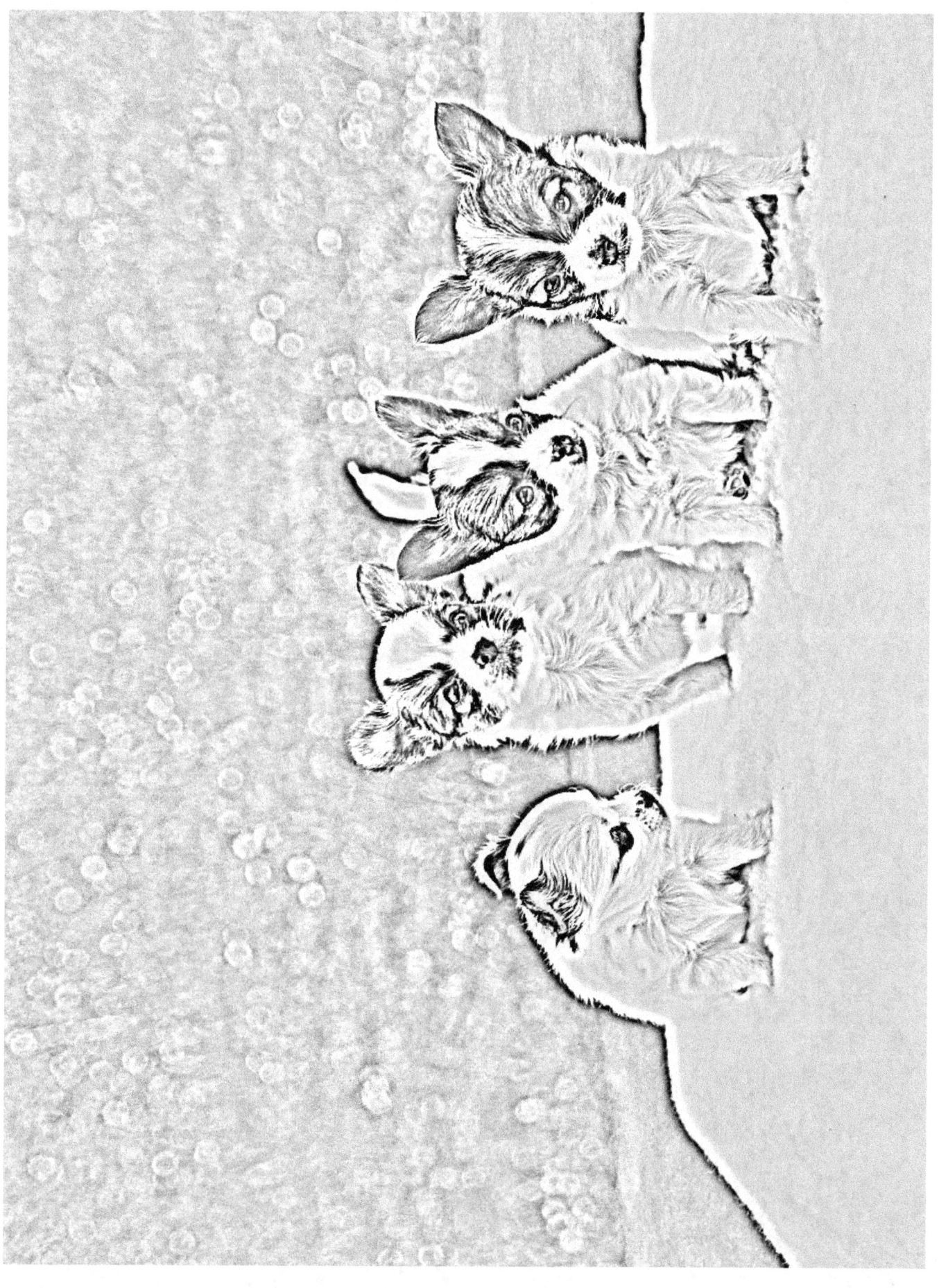

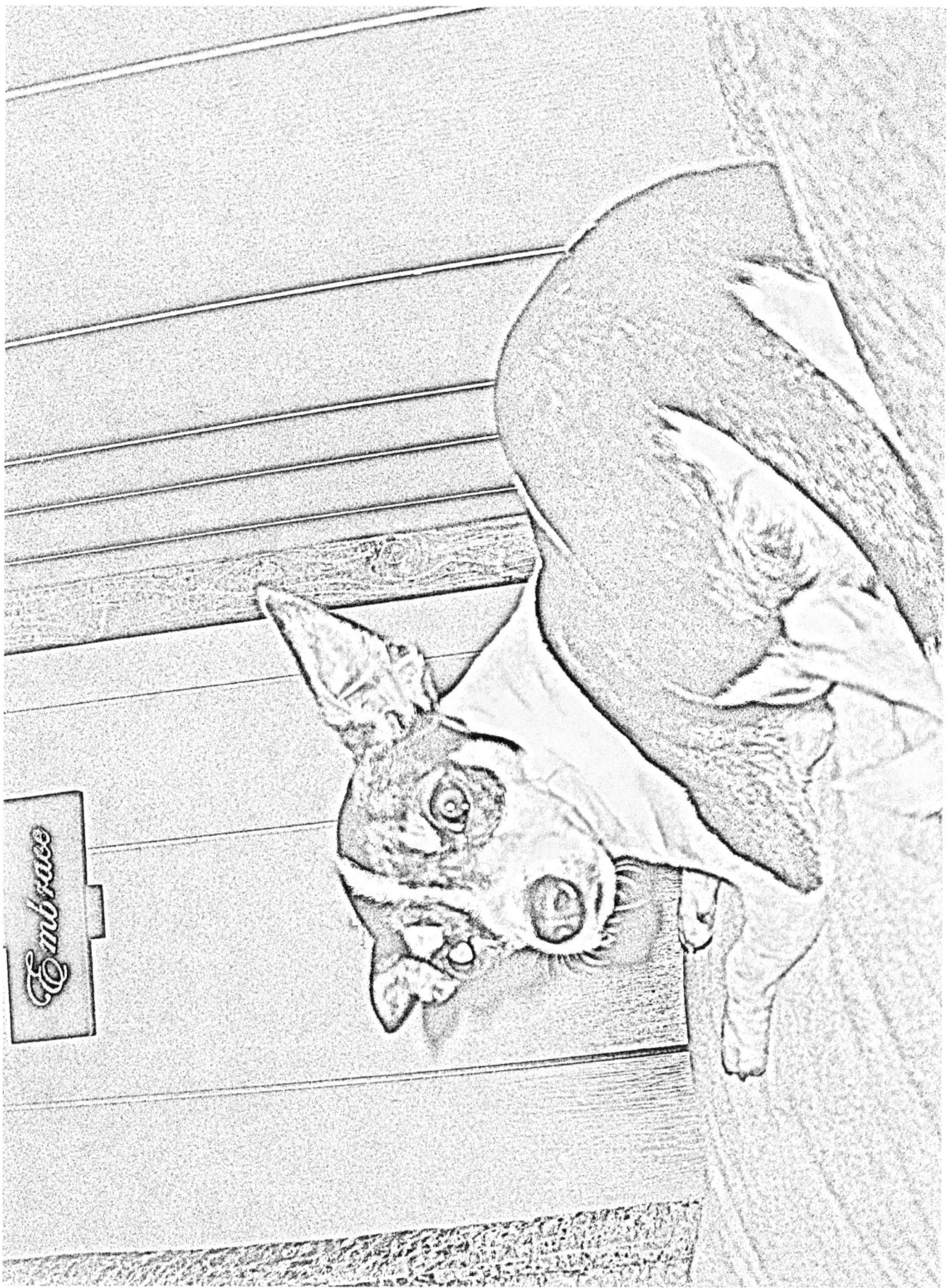

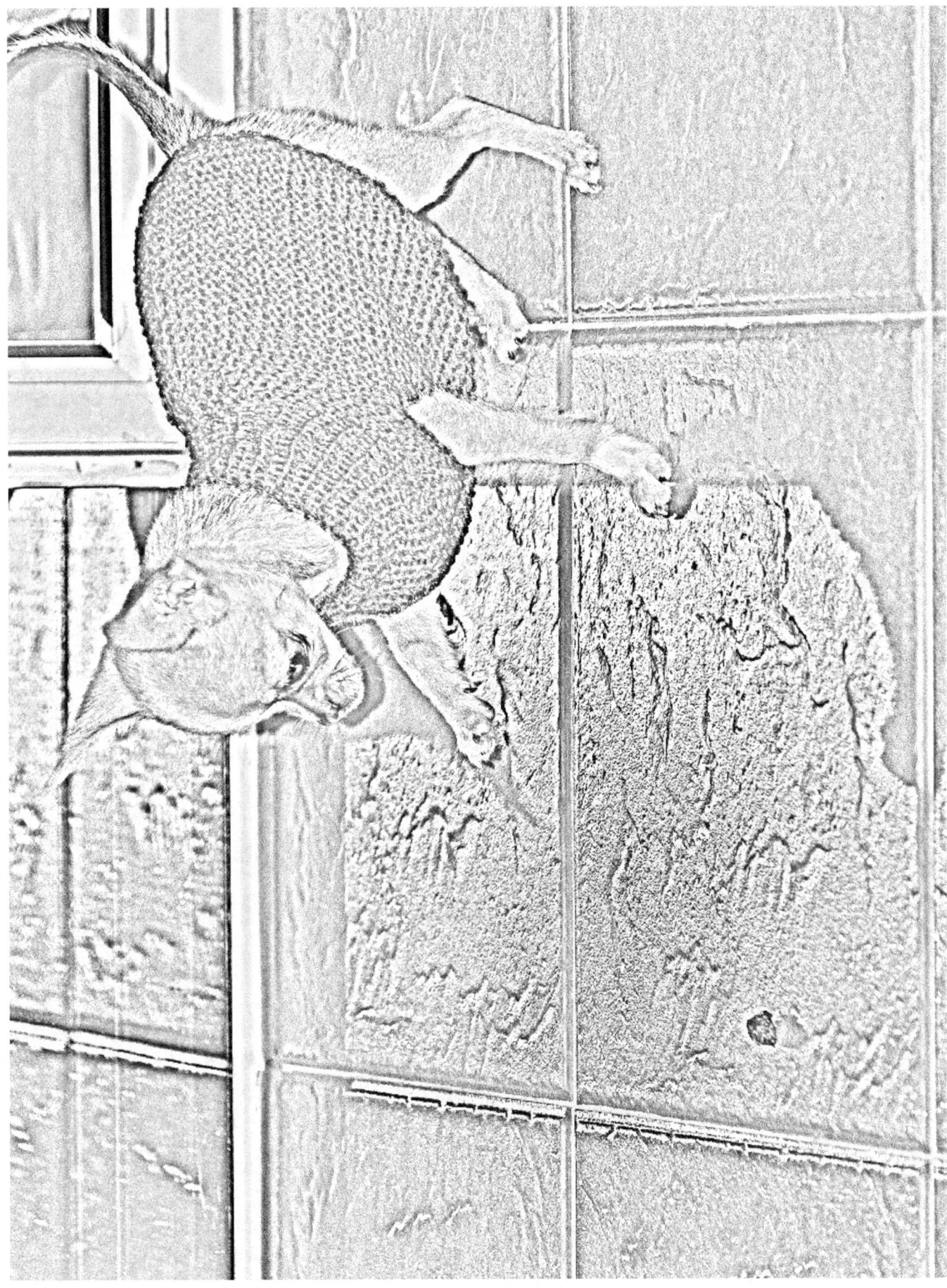

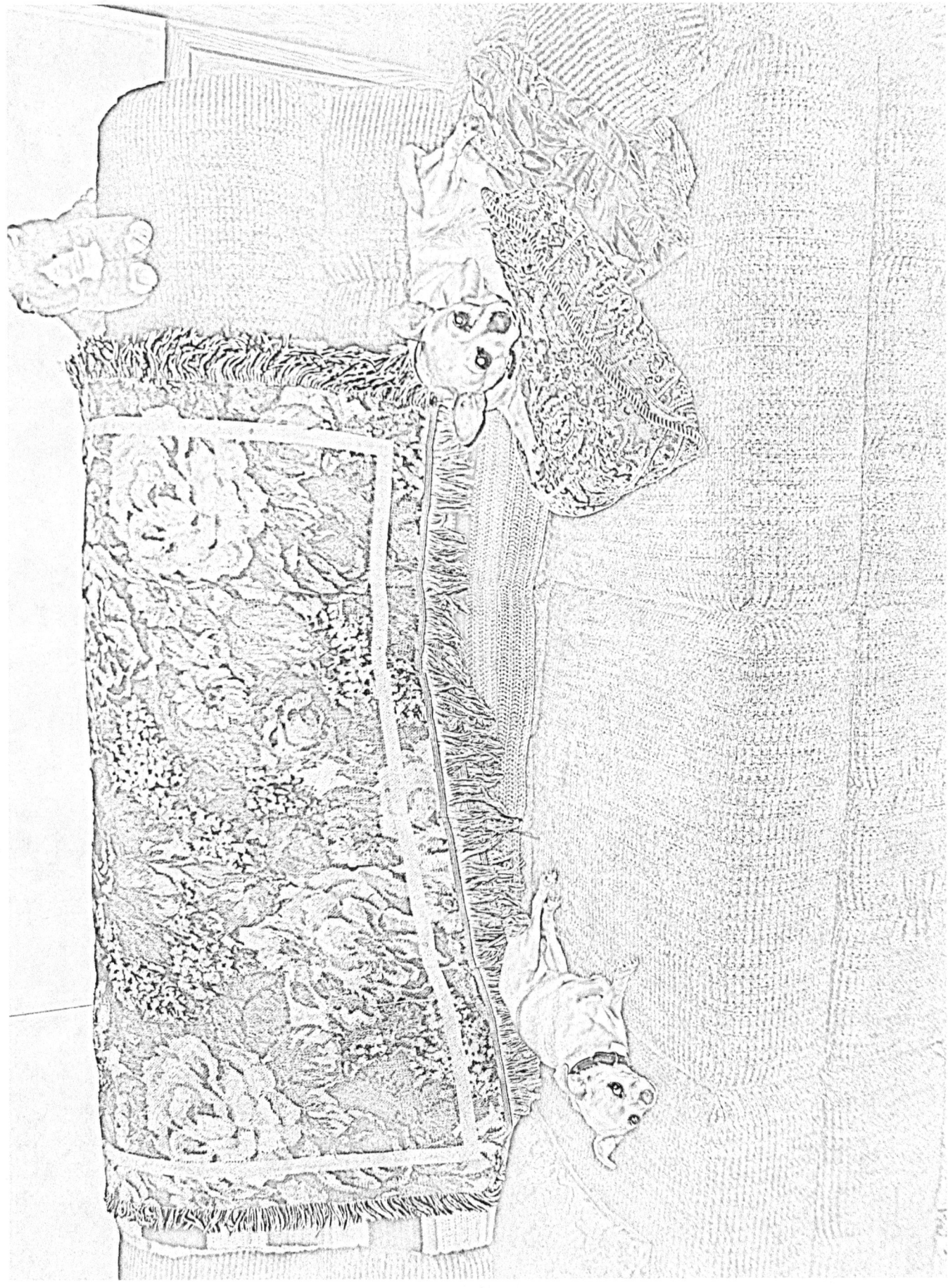

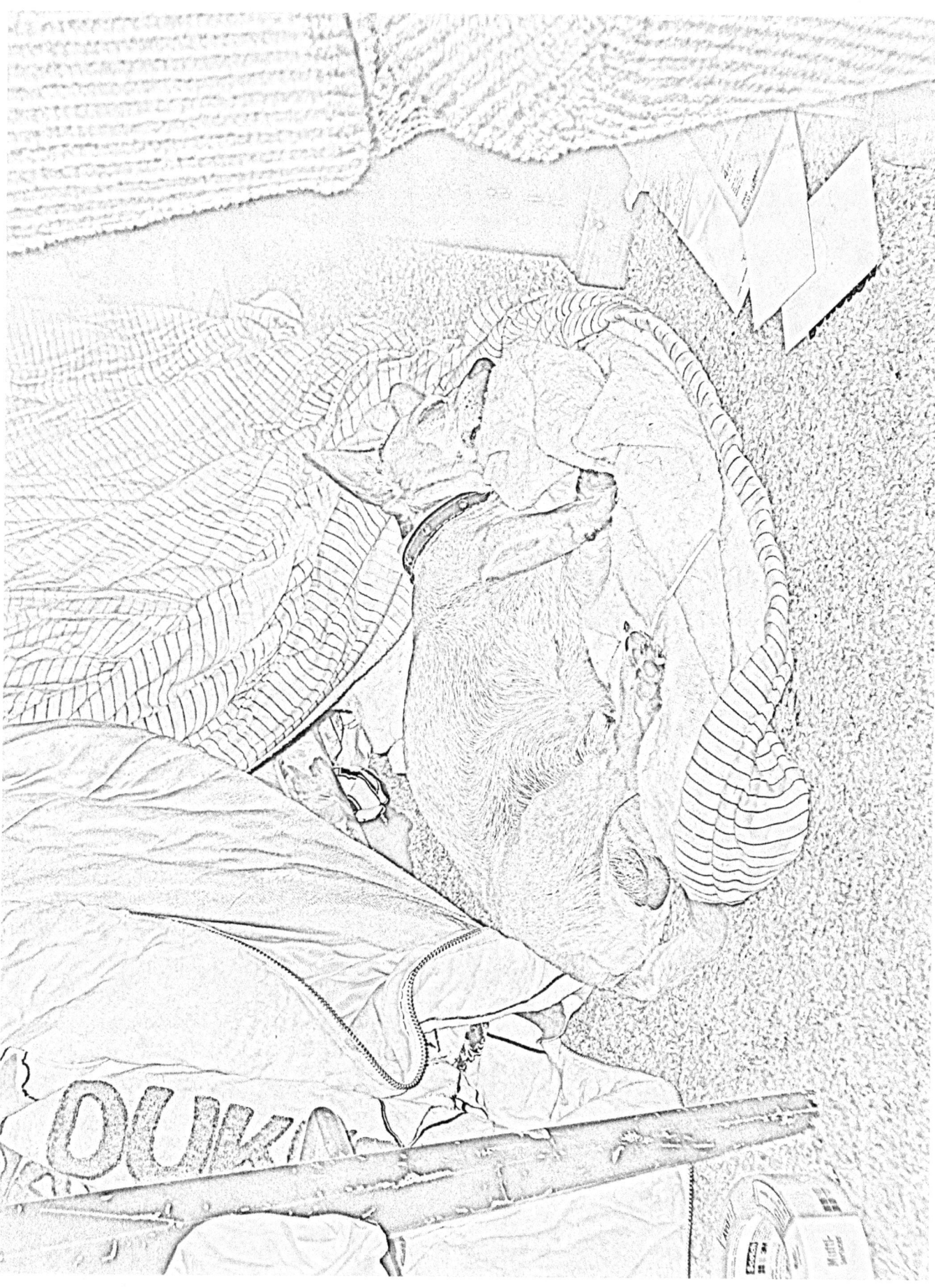

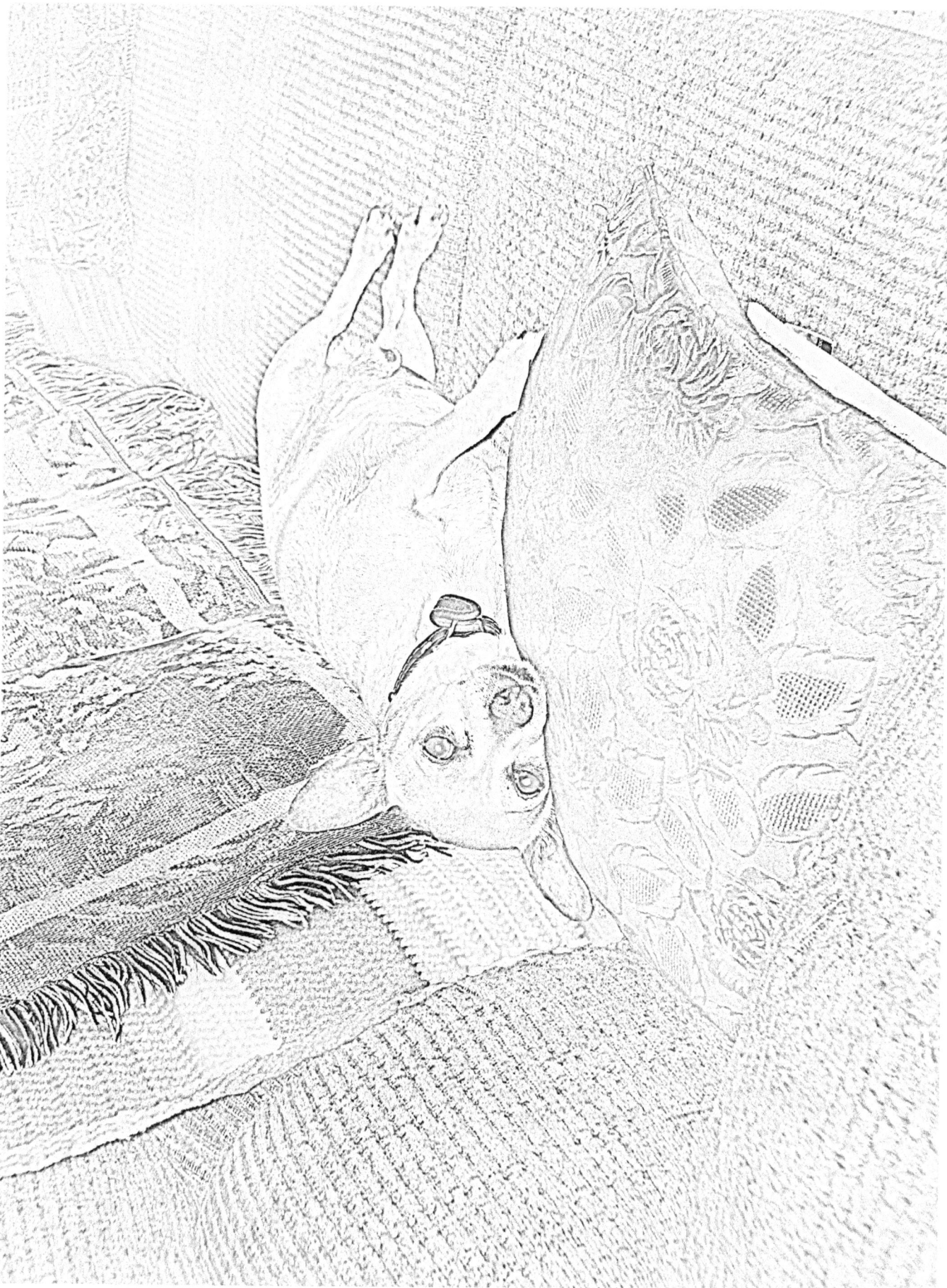

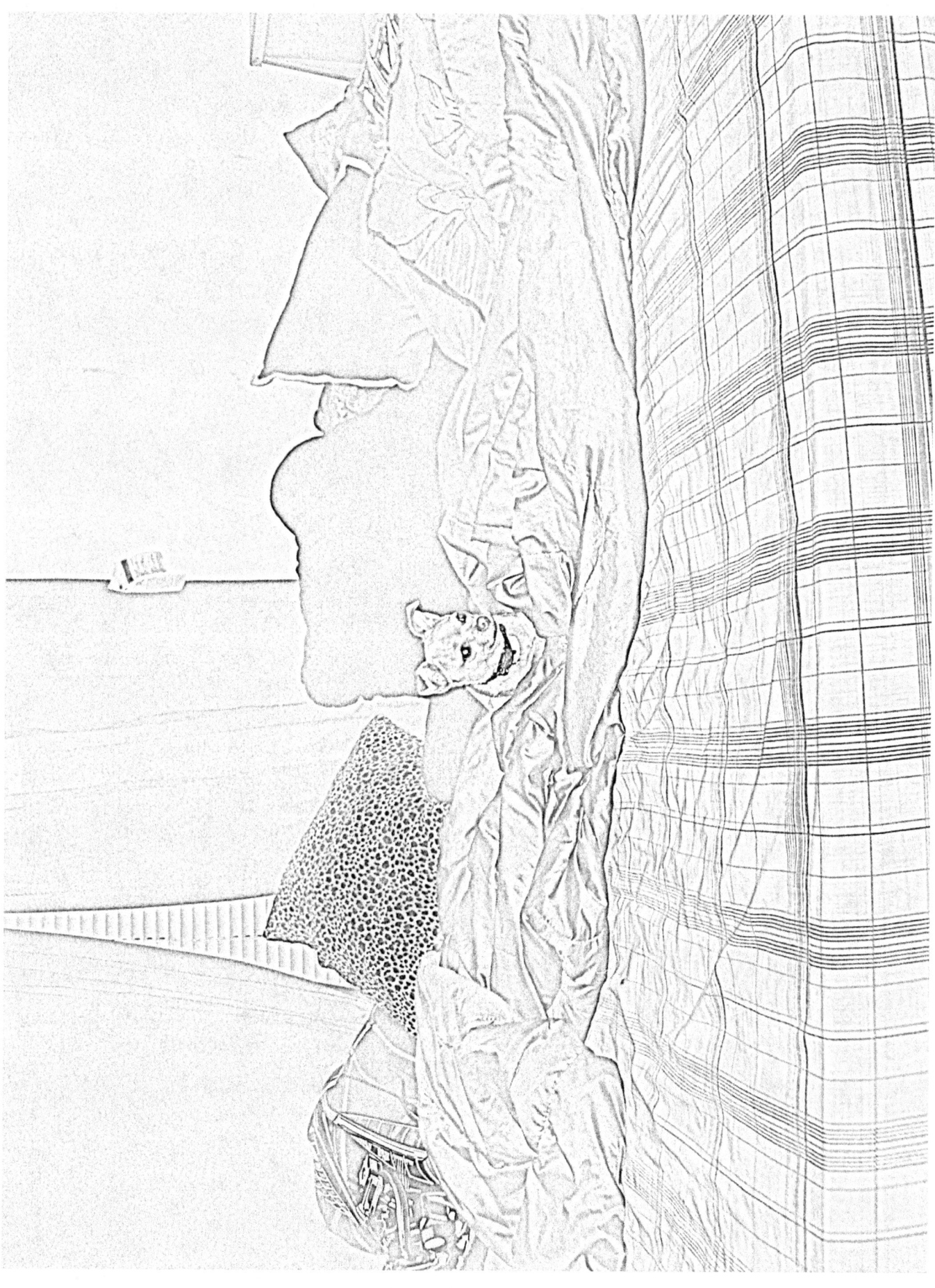

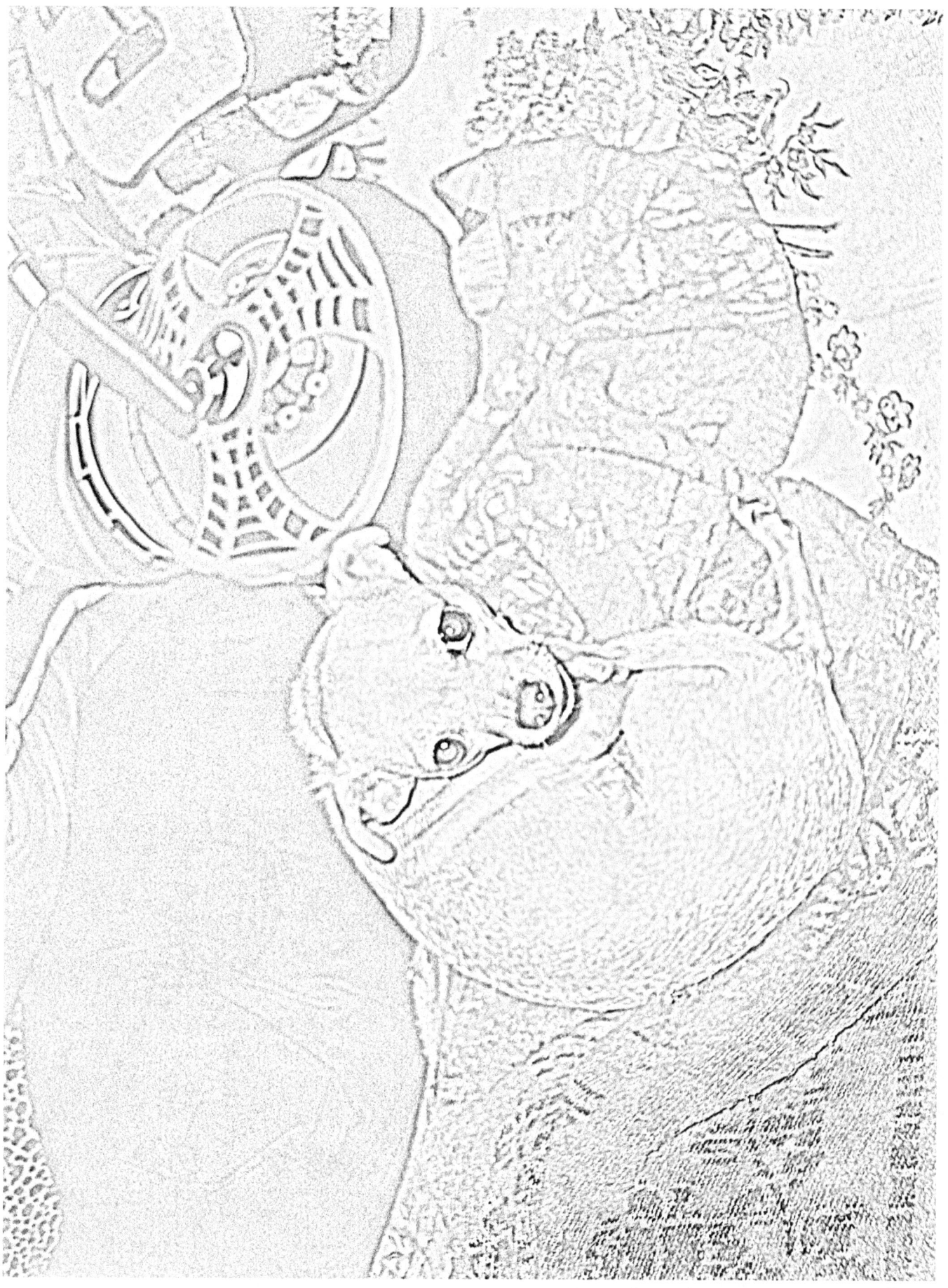

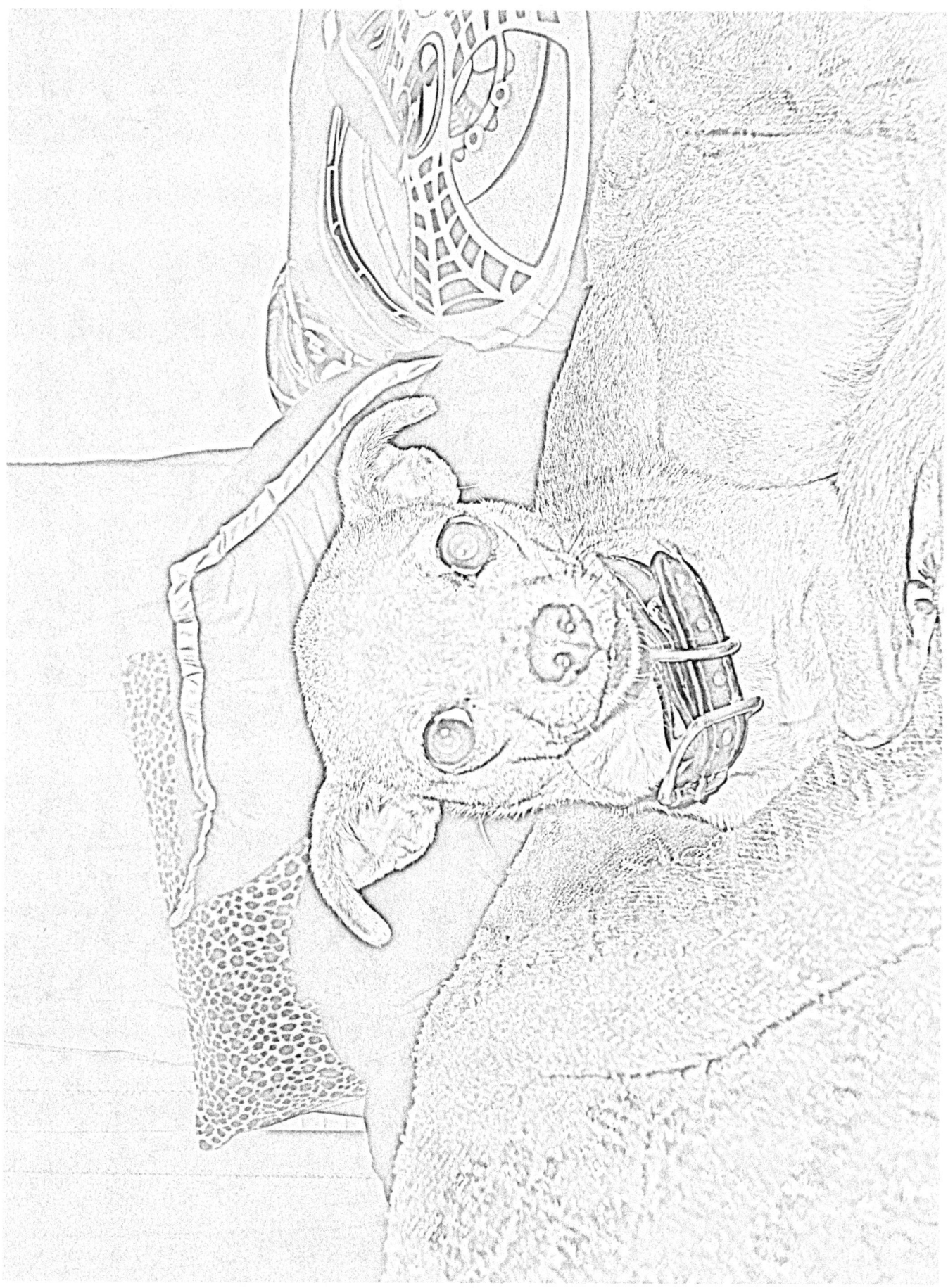

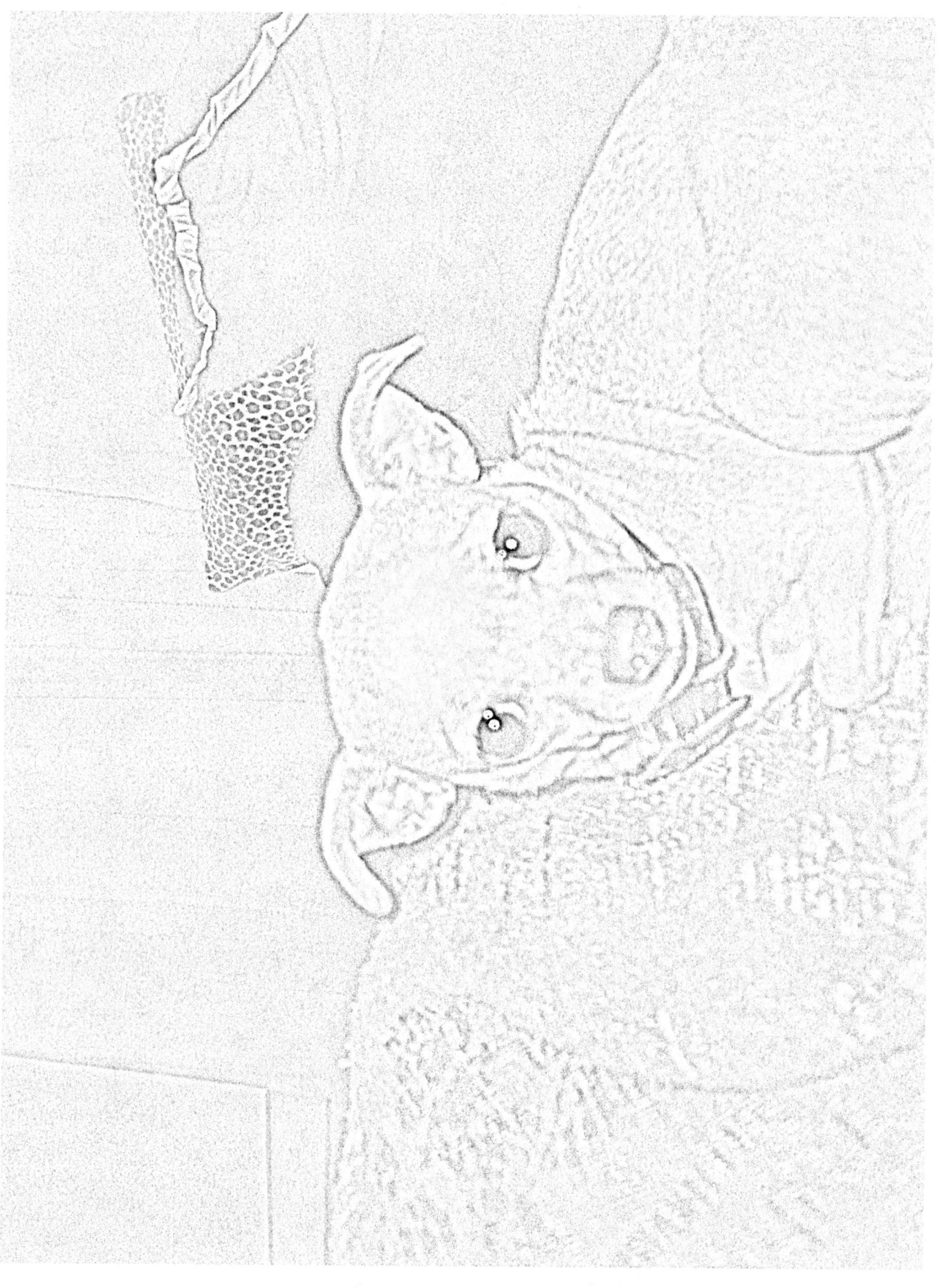

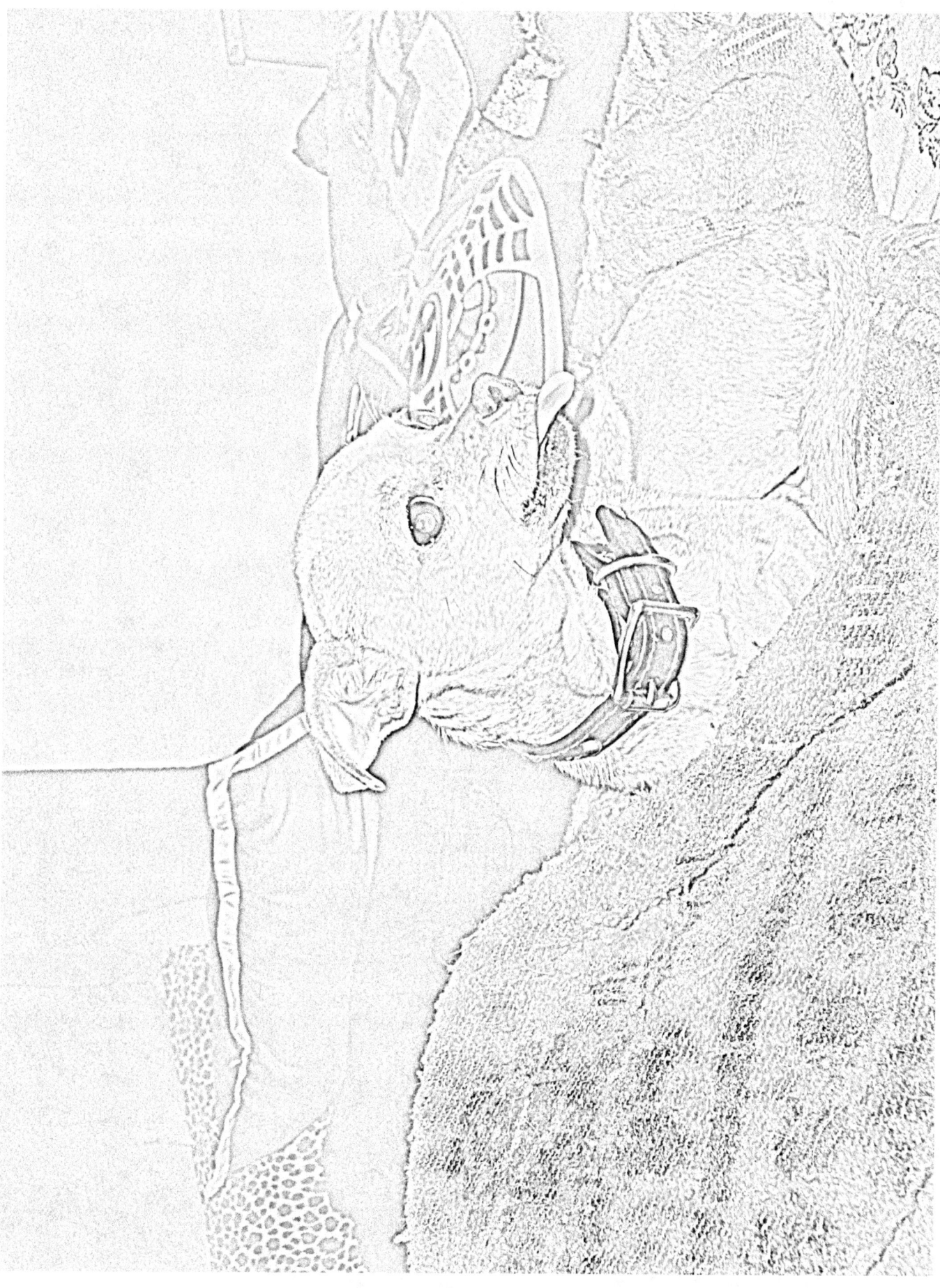

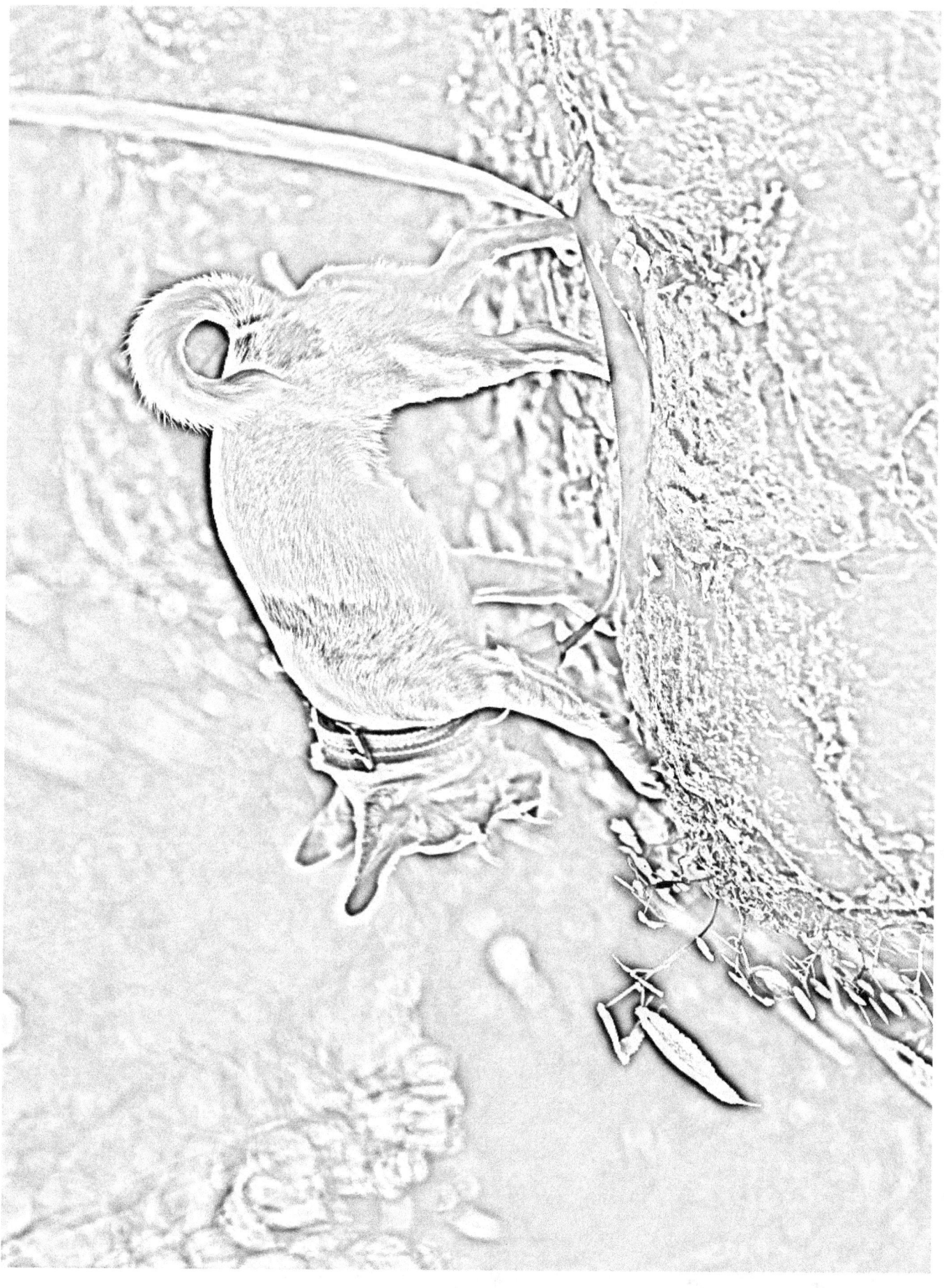

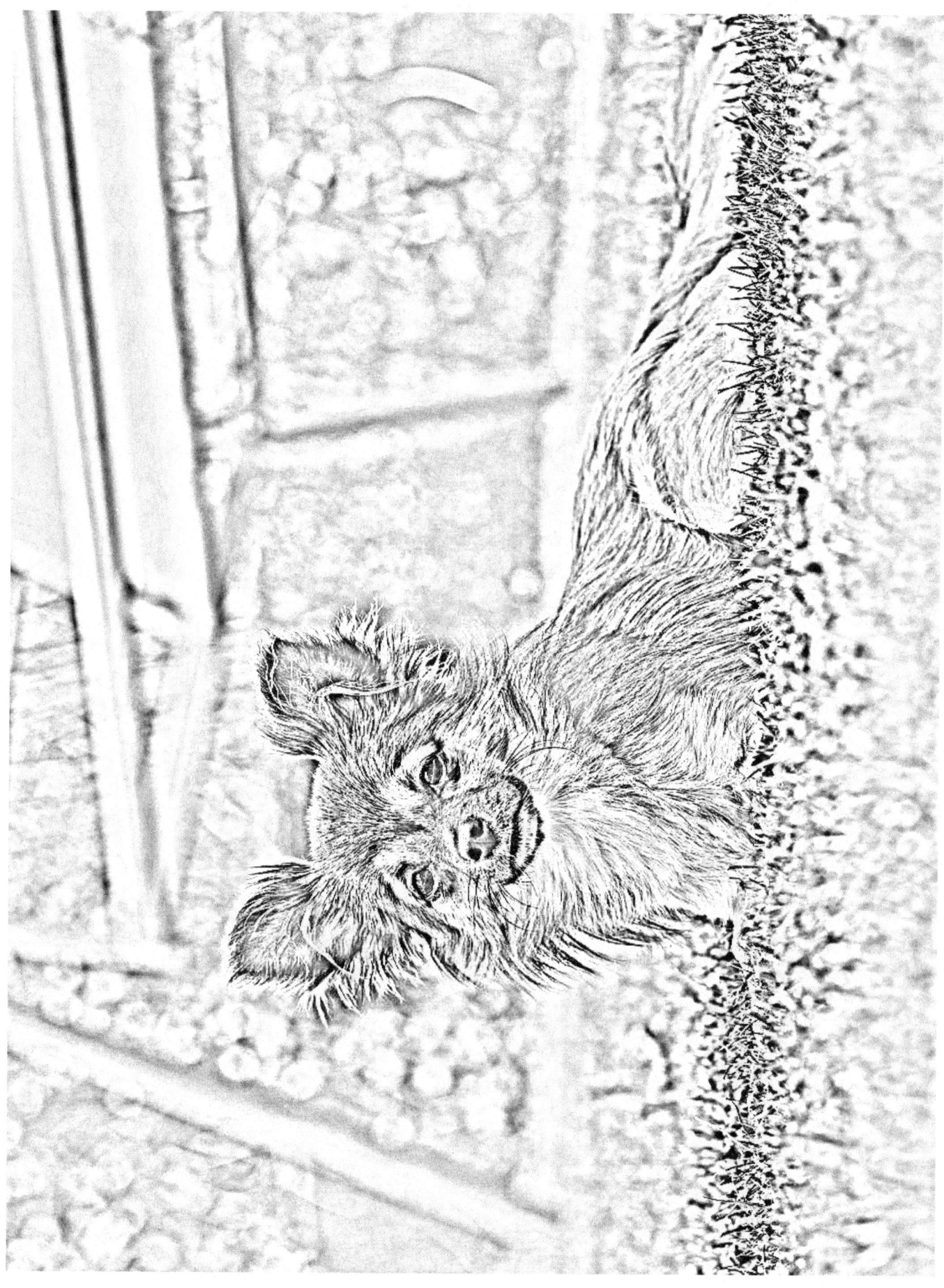

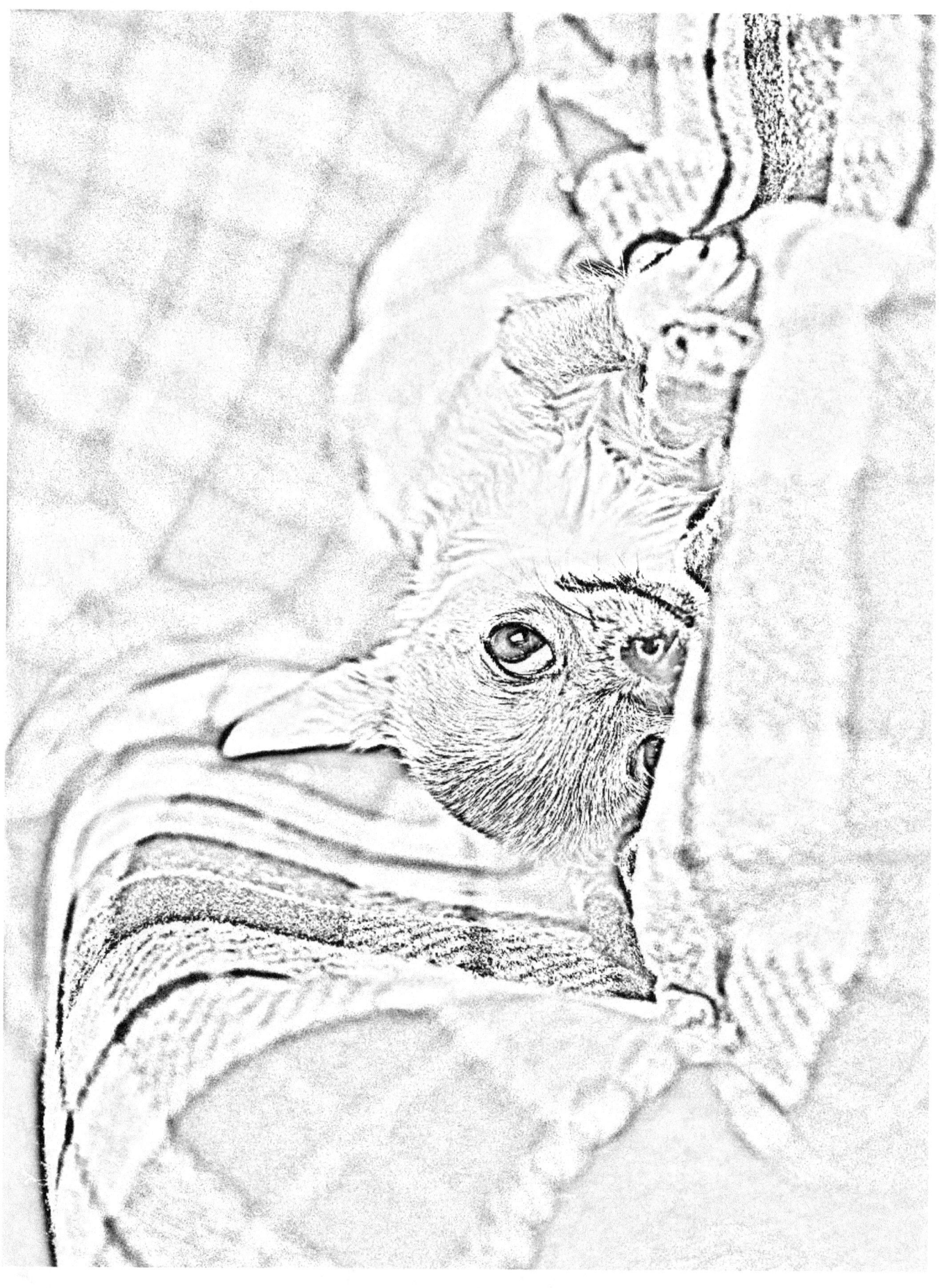

Thank You!
We hope you enjoyed our coloring book.

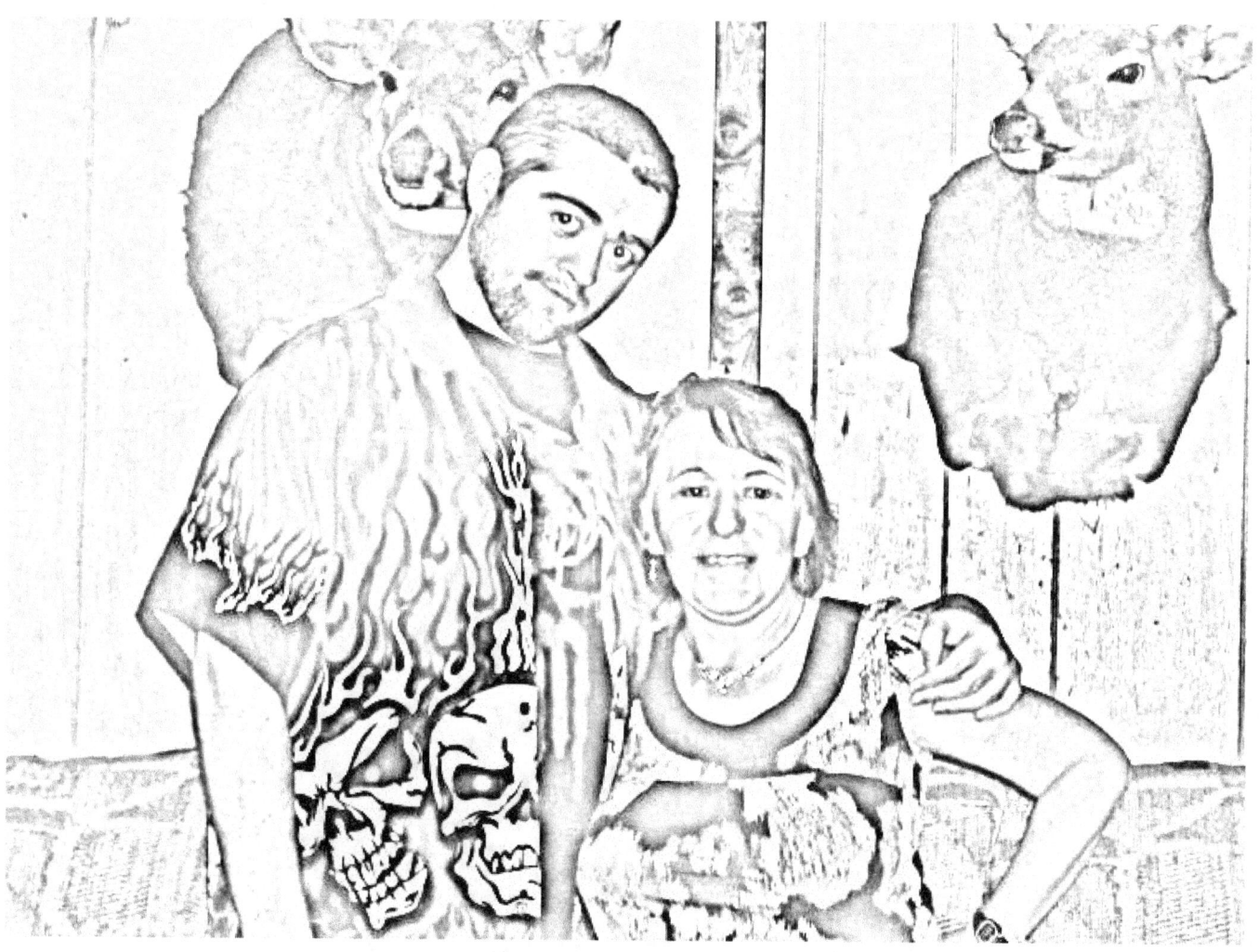

Watch for more color books by A.R.N. Arts LLC.
http://arnarts.wixsite.com/books

www.ingramcontent.com/pod-product-compliance
Lightning Source LLC
Chambersburg PA
CBHW081124180526
45170CB00008B/2999